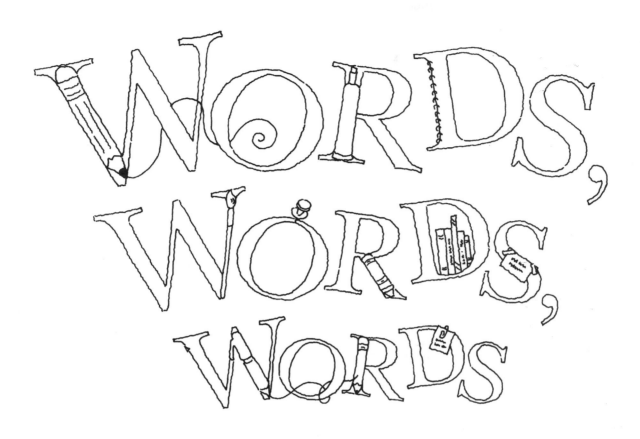

WORDS, WORDS, WORDS

Babs Bell Hajdusiewicz

Good Year Books

Dedication

To Nick and Alison

Good Year Books

are available for most basic curriculum subjects plus many
enrichment areas. For more Good Year Books, contact your local
bookstore or educational dealer. For a complete catalog with
information about other Good Year Books, please contact:

Good Year Books
P.O. Box 91858
Tucson, AZ 85752-1858
www.goodyearbooks.com

Book design and illustration by Amy O'Brien Krupp.

Copyright © 1997 Babs Bell Hajdusiewicz.
All Rights Reserved.
Printed in the United States of America.

ISBN 0-673-36319-8

6 7 8 9 - BN - 06 05 04

Preface

What are some words that mean the same as nice?

Is it's *or* its *the right word to use in your sentence?*

What words rhyme with the word moon?

Words, Words, Words provides the answers to these questions and hundreds more that beginning writers ask as they work to put their ideas on paper.

Words, Words, Words provides a single source where beginning writers can quickly and easily find thousands of words that have been carefully selected and organized in the section "Words, Words, Words." Here, beginning writers have at their fingertips comprehensive lists of synonyms and antonyms, metaphors and similes, homophones and homographs, compound words and contractions, fun words, and more than two-hundred families of rhyming words.

In addition to a glossary and index, *Words, Words, Words* includes proofreader's marks, library classifications, and specialized indexes that help beginning writers find particular synonyms and rhyming-word families.

Whether writing for school assignments or for pleasure, beginning writers will find *Words, Words, Words* an invaluable resource to assist them in becoming the best wordsmiths they can be.

Contents

Kinds of Writing

Did you know that everyone is a writer? It's true. Chances are, before today is over, you will use a pen or pencil or a computer keyboard to write something. Look at some of the reasons you may write.

You want to explain something:

a sign

directions

a caption

rules or instructions

a label

an excuse

a note

a recipe

1

You want to convince someone:

      an advertisement

      an application form

      a sign

      a complaint

You need to ask a question
or get someone's attention:

      a sign

      an announcement

      an advertisement

      a lost or found notice

      an invitation

      a survey

      an interview

      a questionnaire

You want to answer a question:

a definition

an essay

an application

a questionnaire

You want to keep a record of events:

a list

a diary

a journal

a biography

an autobiography

You want to share thoughts and ideas or tell a story:

letter   diary

journal   story

poem   play

joke or riddle   editorial

biography   autobiography

Whether you write a note to a friend, write your thoughts in a diary or journal, make a sign to ask for help in finding a lost pet, or write "This belongs to" and your name on a notebook, you are using words to communicate with yourself or others.

So what words will you choose to use in your writing? And how will you organize these words on paper or the computer screen? The kind of writing you do depends on the words you choose to use and how you choose to use them.

Words,
Words,
Words

Another Way to Say It

(Synonyms, Metaphors, Similes)

Three children describe a runner—but they all use different words! And here are more words that might be used to describe the runner:

She's speedy!

She's like Jackie Joyner-Kersee!

She's a streak of lightning!

Can you think of more ways to describe the runner?

The words <u>quick</u> and <u>speedy</u> are called <u>synonyms</u>. Synonyms are words that mean the same or nearly the same.

The words "a streak of lightning" and "a racehorse" are called <u>metaphors</u>. A metaphor compares one thing to another. The runner's speed is compared to the speed of a racehorse or a flash of lightning.

The words "as fast as a speeding bullet" and "like Jackie Joyner-Kersee" are called <u>similes</u>. A simile uses the words <u>like</u> or <u>as</u> to compare one thing to another. The runner's speed is compared to a bullet's speed or the speed of champion runner Jackie Joyner-Kersee.

Metaphors and similes are <u>figures of speech</u> or <u>figurative language</u>. As a writer, you want your reader to be able to "picture" what you are saying.

So you may want to use synonyms and figures of speech to help you "paint" your pictures.

A <u>cliché</u> is a figure of speech that is used so often that it is said to be "overworked." You could use the cliché "runs like a racehorse" to describe the runner. But your language would be more original if you said the runner was "like a champion sprinter" or "as swift as a cheetah."

You will find many synonyms and figures of speech on the following pages. Basic words are listed alphabetically in dark type. Under each basic word you will find synonyms, metaphors, and similes. You will want to choose the word or words that say exactly what you want to say. You may even want to add some of your own ideas to the lists.

A

alike

equal

like two peas
  in a pod

same

similar

twin

almost

about

around

as good as

close to

for the most
  part

nearly

not quite

angry

about to
  explode

as mad as a
  hornet

at your wit's
  end

boiling

burned up

cross

fed up

fit to be tied

flying off the
  handle

furious

losing your
  temper

like a wild
  animal

mad

mad at the
  world

out of control

seeing red

answer

explain

reply

respond

solve

tell

argue

battle

debate

disagree

lock horns

pick a fight

quarrel

spat

ashamed

embarrassed

guilty

like the
    cat that
    swallowed
    the canary

red-faced

sheepish

ask

beg

call for

inquire

invite

look for

plead

question

request

summon

bad

awful

criminal

crooked

dishonest

evil

harmful

horrible

like yesterday's
    garbage

mean

nasty

poor

rotten

rude

spoiled

terrible

begin

call to order

cut the ribbon

dedicate

dive in

fire away

get going

get the show
    on the road

kick off

open

start

take off

take the first
    step

believe

be convinced

get it through
    your head

have faith in

trust

value

b

big

as big as Texas

awesome

elephant-sized

enormous

gigantic

great

huge

humongous

large

monstrous

outstanding

blame

accuse

bawl out

come down
  hard on

criticize

give a tongue
  lashing

point the
  finger at

scold

tell off

boring

dreary

dull

ho-hum

lifeless

not exciting

pointless

tiring

uninteresting

bother

annoy

bug

disturb

drive you crazy

get under your
  skin

irritate

pester

pick on

tease

brag

blow your own
  horn

boast

pat yourself
  on the back

gloat

show off

sing your own
  praises

brave

courageous

daring

fearless

gutsy

heroic

spunky

unafraid

break

crack

damage

demolish

destroy

pull to shreds

ruin

smash

tear

wreck

bright

brilliant

dazzling

glowing

like a million
   stars

like a newly
   polished
   dance floor

like diamonds

like the
   noonday sun

shiny

sparkling

sunny

build

assemble

construct

create

develop

erect

make

manufacture

mold

produce

burn

char

go up in smoke

scorch

set on fire

smolder

b

busy

active

bustling

involved

no time to
blink

occupied

on the go

racing against
time

working

buy

bargain for

get your hands
on

pay for

pick up

purchase

car

automobile

caboose

convertible

dragster

limousine

streetcar

taxicab

trolley

van

vehicle

carry

bring

cart

deliver

fetch

haul

lug

pass along

take

tote

transport

catch

capture

grab

grasp

hook

net

receive

seize

snatch

trap

celebrate

dedicate

go out on the
    town

honor

kick up your
    heels

observe

whoop it up

change

improve

make over

substitute

switch

trade out

turn color

turn over a
    new leaf

whistle a
    different tune

chase

follow

hunt

pursue

run after

stalk

tag along

track

trail

cheat

con

deceive

do out of

hoodwink

mislead

outwit

pull a fast one

pull the wool
    over your
    eyes

take advantage
    of

trick

choose

adopt

elect

pick

select

vote for

C

clean

bathed
dusted
fresh
laundered
polished
pure
scoured
scrubbed
shiny
sparkling
spick and span
spotless
stainless
swept
tidy
vacuumed
washed

clear

as clear as day
cloudless
like
   handwriting
   on a wall
obvious
plain

cold

an ice cube
bitter
breezy
chilly
cooled
crisp
freezing
frosted
frosty
iced
icy
lifeless
like a witch's
  heart
polar
refrigerated
remote
shivering
unfriendly
windy
wintry

come

appear

approach

arrive

bear down
  upon

gain

reach

show up

turn up

complain

bellyache

bewail

crab

fume

gripe

grouch

grumble

nag

squawk

yammer

confused

at a loss for
  words

baffled

bewildered

buffaloed

can't make
  heads or tails
  of it

disturbed

don't know if
  you're
  coming or
  going

don't know
  which end
  is up

draw a blank

flipped out

flustered

going in circles

in a maze

like a train
  with no
  engine

lost at sea

out of it

spaced out

taken aback

thrown off
  balance

torn

troubled

uncertain

upset

C

Synonyms, Metaphors, Similes

crazy

absurd
batty
bonkers
crazed
dippy
foolish
goofy
has a screw
   loose
    somewhere
idiotic
insane
irrational
loony
lunatic
mad
mad as a
   March hare
nonsensical
not playing
   with a full
   deck

off the wall
out in left field
preposterous
silly
stark raving
   mad
stupid
unbalanced
wacko

crowd

bevy
drove
flock
jam
mob
swarm
throng

cry

bawl
blubber
break down
moan
snivel
sob
wail
weep
whimper
whine

curious

inquiring
inquisitive
investigative
itching to
   know
like a cat
nosy
questioning
searching
snoopy

cut

amputate
carve
dissect
divide
prune
rip
saw
shave
slash
slice
slit
snip
split
tear
trim

D

dangerous

a red light
alarming
chancy
hazardous
like an open
pit
like jumping
into a fire
risky
sounds an
alarm
treacherous
unsafe

dark

dim
dismal
dreary
dull

evil
faint
gloomy
lightless
shadowy

dead

like a corpse
deceased
departed
dormant
extinct
gone
history
inorganic
lifeless
numb
passed away
perished
smothered
suffocated
terminated
tired

d

deep

bottomless

cavernous

in the bowels
   of the earth

like the ocean

way down

different

assorted

contrasting

distinctive

extraordinary

like night
   and day

odd

unique

unlike

unusual

varying

difficult

as clear as mud

exhausting

hard

like beating
   your head
   against a
   brick wall

like being in a
   maze

like finding
   your way in
   the dark

like having
   your hands
   tied behind
   your back

like rowing
   upstream

like trying to
   find a needle
   in a haystack

like trying to
   move
   mountains

mind-boggling

no bed of roses

no picnic

puzzling

tedious

troubling

trying

dirty

dusty
filthy
foul
grimy
a pig sty
a pit
messy
muddy
soiled
spotted
stained
unclean

dry

arid
as dry as a
  bone
bare
boring
dehydrated
like a desert
parched
thirsty
tiresome

E

easy

a cinch
a piece of cake
an ace in the
  hole
all in a day's
  work
elementary
like taking
  candy from a
  baby
like turning on
  a faucet
natural
obvious
like being on
  automatic
  pilot
plain
simple
uncomplicated

21

e

eat

bolt
consume
devour
dine
feast
gobble up
gorge
gulp down
pack it in
pig out
put away
scarf down
snack
stuff your face
wolf it down

empty

a bottomless
  pit
abandoned
blank
deserted
hollow
unfulfilled
unfurnished
vacant

excited

a live wire
alive
all pumped up
anxious about
bustling
can't wait
eager
energetic
enthusiastic
eyes popping
  out
full of steam
full of vim and
  vigor
gung-ho
hyped
keyed-up
like running
  on new
  batteries
worked-up

f

fall

collapse

crumple

drop

go head over
   heels

keel over

sink

slide

slip

slump

stumble

take a
   nose dive

take a spill

topple

trip

tumble

family

ancestors

ancestry

background

bloodline

children

dynasty

folks

heritage

household

kin

pedigree

people

relatives

roots

tribe

famous

a shining star

big cheese

celebrated

distinguished

esteemed

great

king of the
   mountain

popular

respected

top banana

well-known

f

fast

a race horse

as swift as a deer

fleeting

lightning-swift

like a champion sprinter

like a speeding bullet

like a streak of lightning

like Jackie Joyner-Kersee

quick

rapid

speedy

swift

fat

ample

as fat as a pig

big

broad

bulky

chubby

heavy

husky

large

massive

obese

overweight

plump

solid

stout

wide

find

come across

detect

discover

get to the bottom of

locate

notice

pinpoint

solve

spot

turn up

uncover

first

beginning

chief

earliest

foremost

initial

leading

main

major

opening

original

premiere

primary

f

fix

cobble

correct

do up

doctor up

mend

patch

prepare

put right

remedy

repair

restore

solve

straighten

touch up

friend

acquaintance

buddy

chum

classmate

companion

helper

pal

peer

playmate

sidekick

teammate

full

ample

crammed full

crowded

developed

filled

jam-packed

overflowing

packed

stuffed

fun

amusement

delight

enjoyment

entertainment

excitement

like a day with
    your best
    friend

play

pleasure

recreation

f

funny

amusing

bringing down
the house

comical

entertaining

hilarious

humorous

laughable

like a clown

like an
elephant on
stilts

like something
from
"Saturday
Night Live"

ridiculous

side splitting

silly

witty

good

all right

AOK

appropriate

best

correct

delicious

excellent

fine

first class

great

healthful

hits the spot

magnificent

not bad

obedient

okay

outstanding

perfect

praiseworthy

right

safe

suitable

super

superb

superior

takes the cake

tops

trustworthy

well-behaved

well-mannered

grow

add to

become
  greater

bloom

bulge

deepen

develop

double

enlarge

expand

fill out

flourish

germinate

heighten

increase

lengthen

magnify

mature

multiply

prosper

shoot up

snowball

spread

spring up

sprout

stretch

swell

thicken

thrive

widen

H

happy

as happy as a
  lark

at peace with
  the world

blissful

cheerful

contented

delighted

elated

glad

in seventh
  heaven

jolly

joyful

jubilant

lighthearted

like a clam at
  high tide

merry

on cloud nine

on top of the
  world

optimistic

overjoyed

pleased

positive

satisfied

sunny

thrilled

tickled pink

upbeat

walking on air

without a care
  in the world

h

hard

demanding
rigid
set in your ways
stiff as a board
taut
tense
unbending
unyielding

hate

abhor
bear a grudge
  against
can't bear
can't stand
despise
detest
dislike
have no use for
loathe

have

acquire
hold
keep
own
possess

help

aid
assist
boost
come through
do the honors
give a hand
nurse
prevent
rescue
serve
stick together
support
work

high

elevated
heavenly
like a kite
lofty
out of sight
steep
tall
towering

h

hit

bash

beat up

conk

cream

hammer

knock

pound

slap

smack

strike

thump

whack

home

address

apartment

bungalow

cabin

castle

condominium

cottage

hotel

house

pad

residence

shelter

tent

townhouse

trailer

hot

boiling

burning

feverish

fiery

flaming

heated

roasting

sultry

sweating

sweltering

torrid

hungry

famished

hungering

like a
 bottomless pit

like a
 marooned
 sailor

ravenous

starving

h

hurry

accelerate

burn rubber

bustle

fly on the
  wings of
  the wind

get a move on

get cracking

get in gear

go like greased
  lightning

hasten

hightail it

hustle

lose no time

make haste

make hay
  while the
  sun shines

make it snappy

move quickly

race

ride hard

run like mad

rush

scurry

shake a leg

skedaddle

speed

step on the gas

step tall

hurt

abused

broken

bruised

damaged

harmed

injured

like a piece of
  bruised fruit

like a pin
  cushion

feeling like
  you've lost
  your best
  friend

mistreated

pained

ruined

sprained

wounded

interesting

amusing

attractive

charming

enchanting

enjoyable

entertaining

exciting

fascinating

fun

inviting

spellbinding

stimulating

tempting

thought-
   provoking

jealous

desirous

eating your
   heart out

envious

green with
   envy

itching

yearning

join

bind

bridge

connect

consolidate

couple

link

marry

meet

merge

team up

tie

unite

jump

bounce

bound

hop

hurdle

leap

like a kangaroo

like a leapfrog

pounce

spring

vault

j

k

K

keep

preserve

protect

reserve

salvage

save

squirrel away

L

last

all she wrote

caboose

closing

concluding

end

end of the line

ending

final

latest

rearmost

late

behind
 schedule

delayed

overdue

past due

postponed

tardy

laugh

be in stitches

cackle

chortle

chuckle

giggle

guffaw

hoot

howl

make fun of

roar

roll on the
 floor

snicker

split your sides

tee-hee

titter

lazy

a couch potato

idle

inactive

listless

unmotivated

let

admit

allow

approve of

authorize

permit

light

airy

delicate

feathery

like a spider's
 web

nimble

slight

spry

tiny

weightless

little

ant-sized

brief

dinky

dwarfed

itty-bitty

mini

miniature

minor

peewee

scant

short

small

teeny

tiny

wee

lonely

alone

companionless

cut off

forlorn

friendless

haven't a
 friend in the
 world

isolated

lonesome

separate

withdrawn

l

lots

a flood of

a great deal

acres

an army

an excess of

aplenty

as plentiful as
    air

considerable
    amount

enormous
    amount

extra

gobs

heaps

loads

many

masses

more than you
    can handle

mountains of

much

numerous
    quantities

oodles

quite a few

scads

tons

tremendous
    amount

umpteen

volumes

loud

blaring

booming

deafening

earsplitting

earthshaking

fortissimo

harsh

intense

noisy

roaring

thunderous

love

admire

adore

be fond of

be infatuated
    with

care for

cherish

delight in

enjoy

get a kick
    out of

have a liking
    for

hold dear

idolize

like

long for

think the
    world of

treasure

worship

mean

barbaric
bloodthirsty
brutal
cold-blooded
cruel
evil
hateful
hurtful
inhuman
like an old
  buzzard
savage
unfeeling
vicious
wicked

middle

average
bull's eye
center
core
dead-center
focus
heart
hub
like sandwich
  spread
mean
median
midpoint
nucleus

money

bill
bread
bucks
change
coins
deposit
dollar
dough
income
pay
riches
salary
savings
wealth

N

never

at no time

not a fat
chance

hardly ever

not at all

not ever

not in a
million years

rarely

the second
Tuesday of
next week

under no
circumstances

new

contemporary

extraordinary

fresh

hot

latest

modern

recent

unfamiliar

unusual

up-to-the-
minute

nice

a fountain of
kindness

a good egg

agreeable

appropriate

correct

delightful

enjoyable

friendly

good-natured

kind

likable

neighborly

pleasant

polite

proper

right

thoughtful

suitable

night

bedtime

dark

darkness

dusk

evening

nighttime

sunset

twilight

noise

bedlam
commotion
hubbub
hullabaloo
pandemonium
racket
ruckus
turmoil
uproar
yelling

O

often

a lot
every time you
  turn around
frequently
oft
over and over
periodically
regularly
time after time
time and time
  again
usually

old

a dinosaur
a fossil
aged
ancient
antique
as old as
  Methuselah
as old as the
  hills
elderly
extinct
getting on in
  years
old-fashioned
outdated
over the hill
prehistoric
used
worn

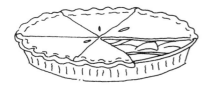

part

chunk
crumb
fraction
part and parcel
particle
piece
portion
scrap
section
segment
share
slice

poor

bankrupt
broke
don't have two
    pennies to
    rub together
financially
    challenged
half-baked
hard up
indigent
needy
penniless
poverty-
    stricken
strapped

pretty

appealing
as lovely as a
    rose
attractive

beautiful
becoming
chic
cool
cute
delightful
eye-catching
fair
fine
glamorous
good-looking
gorgeous
lovely
magnificent
neat
nice
pleasing
striking
stunning
stylish

r

quiet

calm
hushed
like a church
    mouse
on cat feet
passive
peaceful
silent
still
tranquil

ready

about to
agreeable
all set
available
on top of
    things
on your toes
prepared
primed
willing

rich

affluent
loaded
prosperous
rolling in
    dough
wealthy
well-off

right

accurate
correct
exact
fair
fair and square
flawless
honest
just
lawful
legal
licensed
logical
moral
perfect
precise
rational
reasonable
true

r

rough

bumpy
coarse
crinkly
difficult
irregular
jagged
like
   sandpaper
uneven

rub

brush
curry
groom
knead
massage
pat
pet
polish
scour
scrub
smooth
stroke

run

beat it
bolt
canter
dart
dash
depart
flee
gallop
hurry
jog
leave
lope
race
retreat
rush
scamper
scoot
scramble
scurry
speed
sprint
tear out
trot
zoom

S

sad

broken-
hearted
cheerless
crummy
crushed
depressed
discouraged
down in the
dumps
downcast
downhearted

feeling blue
feeling like you
lost your song
feeling like
your bubble
burst
feeling like
your dog just
died
forlorn
gloomy
heartbroken
joyless
let down
miserable
sorrowful
sorry
tearful
unhappy
wearing a long
face

safe

all right
guarded
harmless
home free
in good shape
invulnerable
like money in
the bank
okay
on solid
ground
out of harm's
way
out of reach
out of the
woods
protected
secure
sheltered
undamaged
under lock
and key

S

said

added
admitted
admonished
announced
answered
argued
bawled
bragged
breathed
called
cautioned
challenged
claimed
commanded
commented
cried
croaked
declared
demanded
described
exclaimed
explained

gasped
hinted
informed
laughed
lied
mentioned
mouthed
murmured
offered
ordered
panted
pleaded
praised
preached
promised
proposed
ranted
recited
remarked
reminded
replied
reported
responded

roared
sassed
screamed
shouted
shrieked
sighed
smirked
snapped
spoke
sputtered
stammered
stated
stuttered
suggested
told
uttered
volunteered
warned
wept
whispered
wondered
yelled

saw

beheld

examined

eyed

glanced at

glimpsed

got an eyeful

inspected

kept your eyes
   peeled

laid eyes on

noted

noticed

observed

paid attention
   to

perceived

pictured

realized

sighted

spied

spotted

stared at

surveyed

took note of

understood

viewed

watched

witnessed

scared

a real chicken

afraid

afraid of your
   own shadow

alarmed

as white as a
   sheet

fearful

frightened

getting cold
   feet

hair-raising

horrified

intimidated

like a toddler
   in a haunted
   house

like you've
   seen a ghost

quivering like
   a bowl of jelly

terrified

your hair's
   standing on
   end

S

shiny

bright

clean

glistening

glossy

glowing

like a newly
  polished
  dance floor

polished

radiant

shout

bellow

cheer

cry

exclaim

holler

howl

let off steam

make yourself
  heard

roar

scream

whoop it up

yap

yell

yelp

yip

shy

a clinging vine

apprehensive

bashful

hesitant

meek as a lamb

reluctant

timid

sick

ailing

diseased

ill

unhealthy

unwell

sleep

catch forty
  winks

catnap

conk out

count sheep

crash

doze

get some
  shuteye

grab some Z's

hit the hay

hit the sack

nap

retire

sack out

saw logs

slumber

snooze

zonk out

slow

as slow as a
  seven-year
  itch
dawdling
hesitant
like a sloth
like molasses in
  January
plodding
sluggish
snaillike

smart

a brain
a whiz
as smart as a
  whip
brainy
bright
brilliant
clever
intelligent
keen
knows the
  ropes
like a regular
  computer
like a walking
  encyclopedia
sharp

smooth

flat
like glass
polished
sanded
satiny
seamless

soft

comfortable
cushiony
flexible
like a baby's
  bottom
like cotton
like old leather
plush

steal

cabbage onto
con
hustle
plunder
rip off
rob
shoplift
snitch
swindle
thieve

S

stop

abandon

back off

call it quits

cease

complete

cut off

discontinue

end

finish

give up the
   ship

halt

hit the road

hold your fire

nip in the bud

pull up stakes

put an end to

quit

throw in the
   sponge

wrap up

yield

storm

blizzard

cloudburst

cyclone

downpour

hurricane

monsoon

sandstorm

snowfall

tornado

typhoon

story

adventure

biography

fable

fantasy

folktale

legend

myth

narrative

novel

play

tale

yarn

street

alley

avenue

boulevard

driveway

freeway

highway

lane

pavement

road

route

strip

superhighway

thoroughfare

toll road

turnpike

strong

durable

hardy

Herculean

like an ox

mighty

powerful

rugged

sturdy

tough

suddenly

abruptly

all at once

all of a sudden

before you can say "Jack Robinson"

hurriedly

immediately

in a flash

instantly

on short notice

on the spur of the moment

out of the blue

promptly

quickly

rapidly

speedily

swiftly

without warning

take

accept

acquire

gain

gather

grasp

grip

hold

obtain

pick

possess

receive

t

talk

address

break the news

call the shots

chatter

chatter like a
    monkey

communicate

converse

declare

exchange ideas

express

make a point

pipe up

point out

put in two
    cents worth

rap

say

speak

state

utter

tall

aerial

as tall as the
    Empire State
    Building

elevated

full-grown

high

like Kareem
    Abdul-Jabbar

lofty

towering

thin

all skin and
    bones

as skinny as a
    rail

gaunt

lanky

lean

narrow

pencil-thin

scrawny

skeletal

skinny

slender

slim

threadlike

willowy

wispy

t

tired

beat

bored

bushed

dead to the world

dead-tired

dog-tired

drowsy

exhausted

fatigued

ready to drop

restless

sleepy

spent

tuckered out

weary

wiped out

worn out

true

accurate

authentic

correct

dependable

factual

flawless

genuine

legitimate

natural

nonfictional

official

perfect

proper

real

sincere

tried and true

trusted

truthful

valid

try

attempt

consider

experiment with

give it a whirl

have a go at it

make a stab at it

sample

take a risk

taste

test

think about

try your hand at it

undertake

49

U

ugly

an ugly
    duckling
bad-looking
disfigured
displeasing
hideous
homely
like
    Frankenstein
nasty
repulsive
unappealing
unattractive
unpleasant
unsightly

under

at the bottom
    of
below
beneath
submerged in
underneath

understand

be in the know
catch on
comprehend
deduce
fathom
figure out
get it
get it through
    your head
get the drift of
get the hang of
get the
    message
get the picture
grasp
realize
see the light

very

absolutely

altogether

awfully

by and large

chiefly

completely

considerably

downright

enormously

entirely

especially

exceedingly

extraordinarily

extremely

highly

in particular

mainly

mighty

mostly

particularly

primarily

quite

terribly

thoroughly

to the nth
  degree

totally

uncommonly

uniquely

unusually

walked

ambled

hoofed it

paced

padded

plodded

pranced

roamed

shuffled

strode

strolled

strutted

swaggered

tiptoed

tottered

trekked

trudged

waddled

wandered

went

w

want

be attracted
  to
be in need of
covet
crave
desire
fancy
feel inclined
  toward
feel like
hanker after
have occasion
  for
hope for
hunger for
long for
need
prefer
set your heart
  on
thirst for
wish for
yearn

weak

a pushover
a wet noodle
delicate
diluted
faint
feeble
flimsy
fragile
frail
puny
shaky
unstable

went

abandoned
advanced
ambled

departed
descended
deserted
disappeared
escaped
fled
flew
journeyed
left town
made headway
made off
migrated
passed
proceeded
rambled
ran off
retreated
scrammed
traveled
trekked
vamoosed
wandered
withdrew

W

wet

damp

drenched

humid

like a drowned
  rat

moist

saturated

soaked

soggy

sopping

won

accomplished

achieved

brought home
  the bacon

came in first

came out
  ahead

carried the day

conquered

excelled

gained a
  victory

netted

pulled down

reaped

scored

succeeded

swept

waltzed off
  with

won the
  jackpot

work

assignment

business

career

chore

duty

effort

elbow grease

employment

errand

homework

job

project

schoolwork

task

W

worried

anxious

apprehensive

at loose ends

behind the
   eight ball

concerned

disturbed

fearful

fretful

ill-at-ease

nervous

on edge

on pins and
   needles

troubled

under the gun

uneasy

upset

write

communicate

compose

drop a line

jot

note

pen

record

scribble

wrong

awful

bad

corrupt

criminal

flawed

full of errors

illegal

immoral

improper

inaccurate

incorrect

irrational

mistaken

mixed-up

out in left field

unlawful

untrue

young

a newborn calf

childlike

fresh

immature

minor

new

recent

youthful

Opposites Attract

(Antonyms)

black – white

Antonyms are words that have opposite meanings. Look for a word and its antonym in the alphabetical list below. Can you think of others?

A

above – below
absent – present
add – subtract
adult – child
after – before
against – for
alive – dead
all – none
alone – together
always – never

ancient – modern
answer – question
arrival – departure
ask – tell
asleep – awake
attack – defend
awake – asleep

awake – asleep

B

back – front
backward – forward
beautiful – ugly
before – after
beginning – end
below – above
big – little
birth – death
black – white
boring – exciting
bottom – top
boy – girl
break – repair
bright – dim
buy – sell

C

cause – effect
child – adult
clean – dirty
cold – hot
come – go
cooked – raw
cool – warm
coward – hero
cruel – kind
cry – laugh
curved – straight

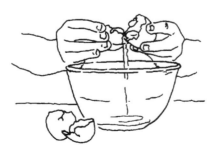

cooked – raw

D

dangerous – safe

dark – light

day – night

dead – alive

death – birth

decrease – increase

deep – shallow

defend – attack

departure – arrival

different – same

difficult – easy

dim – bright

dirty – clean

divorced – married

down – up

dry – wet

dull – shiny

dumb – smart

dwarf – giant

empty – full

E

early – late

earn – spend

east – west

easy – difficult; hard

effect – cause

empty – full

end – beginning

enemy – friend

entrance – exit

even – odd

evening – morning

evil – good

exciting – boring

exit – entrance

F

fact – fiction
fail – pass
false – true
fancy – plain
far – near
fast – slow
female – male
few – many
fiction – fact
find – lose
finish – start
first – last
float – sink
follow – lead
foolish – wise
for – against
forget – remember
forward – backward

from – to

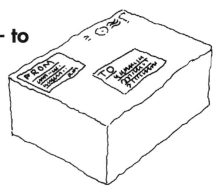

friend – enemy
from – to
front – back
frozen – melted
full – empty

G

giant – dwarf
give – receive
go – come; stop
good – evil
guilty – innocent

happy – sad
hard – easy
hard – soft
hate – love
heavy – light
hero – coward
high – low
hot – cold

real – imaginary

I

imaginary – real
increase – decrease
innocent – guilty
inside – outside

heavy – light

J

joy – pain

K

kind – cruel

59

L

little – big

large – small
last – first
late – early
laugh – cry
lead – follow
learn – teach
least – most
left – right
less – more
light – dark
light – heavy
little – big
loose – tight
lose – find
lost – won
love – hate
low – high

M

male – female
many – few
married – divorced
melted – frozen
messy – tidy
modern – ancient
more – less
morning – evening
most – least

N

narrow – wide
near – far
never – always
new – old
night – day
no – yes
noisy – quiet
none – all
north – south

P

pain – joy
pass – fail
plain – fancy
play – work
polite – rude
poor – rich
present – absent
private – public
pull – push

O

odd – even
off – on
old – new; young
open – shut
outside – inside
over – under

present – absent

Q

question – answer
quiet – noisy

R

raw – cooked
real – imaginary
receive – give
remember – forget
repair – break
rich – poor
right – left
rough – smooth
rude – polite

S

sad – happy
safe – dangerous
same – different
sell – buy
serious – silly
shallow – deep
shiny – dull
short – tall
shout – whisper

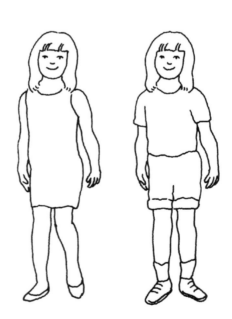

same – different

shut – open

sick – well

silly – serious

sink – float

sit – stand

slow – fast

small – large

smart – dumb

smooth – rough

soft – hard

sour – sweet

south – north

spend – earn

stand – sit

start – finish

stop – go

straight – curved

subtract – add

sunrise – sunset

sweet – sour

tall – short

tame – wild

teach – learn

tell – ask

thick – thin

tidy – messy

tight – loose

to – from

together – alone

top – bottom

true – false

teach – learn

ugly – beautiful
under – over
up – down

warm – cool

well – sick

west – east

wet – dry

whisper – shout

white – black

wide – narrow

wild – tame

wise – foolish

won – lost

work – play

yes – no
young – old

young – old

They Look the Same, But . . .

(Homographs)

O I N K

pen with oink

pen with ink

The words <u>pen</u> and <u>pen</u> look alike. But they have very different meanings! Words that are spelled alike but have very different meanings are called <u>homographs</u>.

TIP: It is easy to remember that homographs are words that <u>look</u> the same. Just think about a graph—you <u>look</u> at a graph.

Here are some homographs and their meanings. Can you think of others?

b

ball   That dog ran off with the <u>ball</u>.
(round object)

My parents went to the holiday <u>ball</u>.
(formal dance)

band   The marching <u>band</u> played at the game.
(group of musicians)

The <u>band</u> is missing from my hat.
(thin strip around)

bank   I put my money in the <u>bank</u>.
(a business place)

We fished along the <u>bank</u>.
(edge along a river)

bark   The tree is missing
some <u>bark</u>.
(tree covering)

She'll <u>bark</u> when
someone comes.
(dog's noise)

b

bat   We saw a <u>bat</u> in our attic. (animal)

Who will <u>bat</u> first? (strike a ball)

The baseball players used my <u>bat</u> for practice. (club)

batter   Andy is the first <u>batter</u>. (baseball player)

The cake <u>batter</u> is good. (uncooked mixture)

bay   Dad put a <u>bay</u> leaf in the stew. (leaf used in cooking)

We live near the <u>bay</u>. (part of a sea)

bill   Dad paid the <u>bill</u>. (statement of what is owed)

The bird's <u>bill</u> was stuck. (beak)

b

bit   May I have a <u>bit</u> of that? (small piece)

Mom bought a new <u>bit</u> for the drill.
(pointed tool)

Murphy <u>bit</u> into a bad apple. (did bite)

bow   I would <u>bow</u> before a king.
(bend in respect)

The <u>bow</u> is sinking. (front of a ship)

bow   My little sis wears a <u>bow</u> in her hair.
(looped ribbon)

I have a <u>bow</u> and no arrows.
(wood weapon)

bowl   Put some cereal
in a <u>bowl</u>. (deep dish)

I like to <u>bowl</u>. (a game)

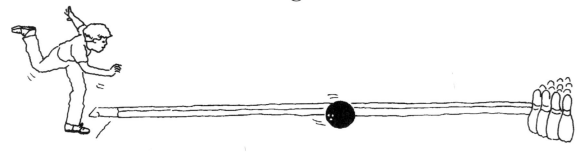

C

box   Please put it in a <u>box</u>. (container)

Phil will <u>box</u> tonight. (sport with gloves)

bridge   We drove over a long <u>bridge</u>. (crossover)

My grandma
plays <u>bridge</u>. (card game)

can   We <u>can</u> see a cave. (are able to)

I need a <u>can</u> of orange paint. (container)

count   My sister is learning to <u>count</u>. (number items in order)

Your opinion doesn't <u>count</u>. (have worth)

Randolph is a <u>count</u>. (nobleman)

C

crow   A <u>crow</u> is in that tree.
(large bird)

The rooster's
<u>crow</u> woke me.
(loud cry)

This is nothing to <u>crow</u> about.
(slang for <u>brag</u>)

My uncle is descended
from the <u>Crow</u>.
(Native-American tribe)

date   What is today's <u>date</u>? (specific day)

We have a <u>date</u> tomorrow.
(planned meeting)

I do not want to eat a <u>date</u>.
(fruit of a date palm)

down   We went <u>down</u> the stairs. (a lower place)

I like a <u>down</u> pillow. (soft feathers)

This is the third <u>down</u>. (football term)

ear   My <u>ear</u> hurts.
(hearing organ)

I ate an
<u>ear</u> of corn.
(part of a plant)

fair   We're going to the county <u>fair</u>. (event)

That's not <u>fair</u>! (equal; just)

Today's weather is <u>fair</u>. (clear and sunny)

She is <u>fair</u>-haired. (light)

fan   The <u>fan</u> helps keep us cool.
(blowing machine)

My mom is a Celtics <u>fan</u>. (admirer)

file   Help me <u>file</u> these papers.
(put away orderly)

I need a new <u>file</u>. (drawer; folder)

She uses a <u>file</u> on her fingernails.
(a manicure tool)

f

fine   That is <u>fine</u> with me. (okay)

My brother paid my library <u>fine</u>. (money as penalty)

fit   This shirt won't <u>fit</u> me! (right size)

My two-year-old brother had a <u>fit</u>. (tantrum)

flat   The land is <u>flat</u>. (not hilly)

Our <u>flat</u> is on the second floor. (apartment)

fly   The bird can't <u>fly</u>. (soar through air)

A <u>fly</u> is on the table. (insect)

ground   We sat on the <u>ground</u>. (soil; earth)

Mom cooked <u>ground</u> turkey. (minced by grinding)

h

gum   There's <u>gum</u> stuck on my shoe.
(chewing substance from trees)

My <u>gum</u> is bleeding. (tissue around teeth)

hatch   Please close
the <u>hatch</u>.
(a cover)

The chicks might
<u>hatch</u> today.
(be born)

heel   I broke my <u>heel</u>.
(rear bottom of shoe or foot)

My dog will <u>heel</u> when I walk him.
(stay close behind)

The boat might <u>heel</u>. (tip to one side)

hide   I can't <u>hide</u> my feelings.
(keep from showing)

They made things from <u>hide</u>.
(animal skin)

j

jam   I like <u>jam</u> on peanut butter.
(sweet preserve)

We had to <u>jam</u> the things in. (pack tightly)

We sat in a traffic <u>jam</u>. (crowd)

jumper   Nancie wore a <u>jumper</u>
to school.
(type of garment)

My cat is a <u>jumper</u>.
(one who jumps)

kind   I try to be <u>kind</u>. (good-natured)

What <u>kind</u> of animal is that? (type)

lap   I will run one
<u>lap</u> with you.
(course traveled)

This kitty loves
my <u>lap</u>.
(upper legs when sitting)

1

last	You won't be <u>last</u>. (at the end)
	This will never <u>last</u>. (go on and on)
lead	We <u>lead</u> the others. (did lead; guided)
	There's no <u>lead</u> in my pencil. (soft graphite)
left	There's no food <u>left</u>. (remaining)
	Put it on the <u>left</u> side. (opposite of right)
	We <u>left</u> the concert. (did leave)
lie	I would never <u>lie</u> about this. (tell an untruth)
	I need to <u>lie</u> down. (stretch out flat)
light	This <u>light</u> is too bright. (ray of energy)
	The feathers are <u>light</u>. (not heavy)
	The bird might <u>light</u> on my head! (land)

like   This is <u>like</u> a dream. (similar to)

I <u>like</u> you. (am pleased with)

line   There's a <u>line</u> all the way to the street. (single row)

I helped Mom <u>line</u> the drawers. (cover insides)

We have a fax <u>line</u>. (wire circuit)

loaf   I can't afford to <u>loaf</u>. (be idle)

I'll buy a <u>loaf</u>. (bread shape)

lock   Please <u>lock</u> up when you leave. (fasten the entrance)

Mom saved a <u>lock</u> of my hair. (piece)

long   I <u>long</u> for recess time. (wish for)

It's a <u>long</u> way away. (great length)

mail   The <u>mail</u> hasn't come yet. (letters)

I'll <u>mail</u> it tomorrow. (send)

My brother tried to make a suit of <u>mail</u>. (armor)

mat   Leave it under the <u>mat</u>. (small rug)

I like the <u>mat</u> on that picture. (border)

My dog's hair will <u>mat</u> if it gets wet. (tangle)

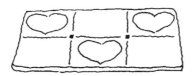

match   These clothes don't <u>match</u>. (go together)

The tennis <u>match</u> is tonight. (planned contest)

Don't strike that <u>match</u>! (stick that makes fire)

mean   He is not a <u>mean</u> person. (unkind)

I didn't <u>mean</u> that! (intend)

m

miss   I <u>miss</u> my best friend. (long for)

<u>Miss</u> Thomas is my teacher.
(unmarried woman's title)

I hope I don't miss! (fail to hit target)

mole   I have a <u>mole</u> on my arm.
(brown skin spot)

There is a <u>mole</u> living in our yard.
(small animal)

palm   My <u>palm</u> itches!
(inside of hand)

The <u>palm</u> is
growing nicely.
(kind of tree)

peck   Birds sometimes <u>peck</u> at our windows.
(strike at with bill)

Who picked a <u>peck</u> of pickles?
(a measured amount)

pen   The <u>pen</u> won't
hold that horse.
(enclosed area)

I need some
paper and a <u>pen</u>.
(writing instrument)

pitcher   Please pass the <u>pitcher</u> of lemonade.
(jar with spout)

Who's the <u>pitcher</u> for your team?
(player who pitches)

pool   The <u>pool</u> water is cold. (tank of water)

We played <u>pool</u> at my house. (table game)

Let's <u>pool</u> our money. (put together)

pop   I heard it <u>pop</u>. (quick, short sound)

My <u>pop</u> says I can go. (dad)

I like some kinds of <u>pop</u>. (soft drink)

I like <u>pop</u> art. (popular)

p

pound Please get a <u>pound</u> of beans. (unit of weight)

We got our dog at the <u>pound</u>. (pen)

I'll <u>pound</u> on your door to wake you. (hit hard)

present I need to take a <u>present</u>. (gift)

Everyone is <u>present</u> today. (not absent)

pupils Our class has two new <u>pupils</u>. (students)

Your <u>pupils</u> are so tiny. (black part of eye)

rest We ate the <u>rest</u> of the pizza. (what is left)

I like to <u>rest</u> after I run. (relax)

ring My sister has a class <u>ring</u>. (finger jewelry)

Did you hear it <u>ring</u>? (bell sound)

Elephants marched in the <u>ring</u>. (circle)

root   I will <u>root</u>
for you!
(cheer)

The <u>root</u>
is showing.
(plant's support)

row   You need to help me <u>row</u>.
(move using paddles)

I stood in the second <u>row</u>. (line)

saw   I <u>saw</u> the accident. (did see)

This <u>saw</u> is dull. (cutting tool)

school   I'll go to a new
<u>school</u> next year.
(place to learn)

A <u>school</u>
of fish
raced by.
(group)

S

seal   My paper has an official <u>seal</u>.
          (mark of approval)

          The sea lion is one kind of <u>seal</u>.
          (sea mammal)

second   Please wait a <u>second</u>. (part of a minute)

          I was <u>second</u> in line. (number two)

slip   I'll <u>slip</u> into my seat. (move easily)

          You'll need this <u>slip</u> to get back in class.
          (paper)

          Mom's <u>slip</u> was showing. (underskirt)

slug   She might <u>slug</u> her brother. (hit hard)

          There's a <u>slug</u> on the porch.
          (kind of snail)

sock   One <u>sock</u> is
          always missing. (footwear)

          I will <u>sock</u> the ball!
          (hit hard)

story   His office is on the fifth <u>story</u>.
(building's floor)

Tell me a bedtime <u>story</u>. (tale)

tick   The clock won't <u>tick</u>. (sound)

My dog had a <u>tick</u>
on his ear. (kind of insect)

toll   You'll hear the <u>toll</u> every hour.
(bell sound)

We'll have to pay a <u>toll</u> every ten miles.
(fee for using)

top   The baby giggled when she
saw the <u>top</u>. (spinning toy)

That cat is on <u>top</u> of the cupboard.
(highest place)

well   I don't feel <u>well</u>. (good)

My uncle's farm has a <u>well</u>.
(hole as source of water)

y

yard I need a <u>yard</u> of ribbon. (three feet)

My dog will not stay in the <u>yard</u>.
(grassy area)

They Sound the Same, But . . .

(Homophones)

"My big sister's ring is a whole **carat!**"

"A whole **carrot**? Wow! I've gotta see that!"

"That's not a **carrot!**"

The words <u>carrot</u> and <u>carat</u> sound alike. But they are not spelled alike. And they have very different meanings! Words that sound alike but are spelled differently and have very different meanings are called <u>homophones</u>.

TIP: It is easy to remember that homophones are words that <u>sound</u> the same. Just think of a telephone—you hear <u>sounds</u> when you use a phone.

Here are some homophones and their meanings. Can you think of others?

a

ad means an advertisement.

I read an <u>ad</u> in the newspaper.

add means to put numbers together.

He can <u>add</u> all the numbers.

aisle means a pathway.

The bride is coming

down the <u>aisle</u>.

I'll means I will. <u>I'll</u> be there in a minute.

isle means an island.

We'll take a ferry

to the <u>isle</u>.

all ready means to be prepared.

I was <u>all</u> ready to go an hour ago!

already means earlier. I <u>already</u> brushed the dog.

allowed means to receive permission.

I'm not <u>allowed</u> to stay up late.

aloud means out loud. Please read that <u>aloud</u>.

b

ant means an insect.

Mom found a carpenter <u>ant</u> in the drawer.

aunt means a female relative.

My <u>aunt</u> is coming to visit.

ate means to have eaten in the past.

Raoul <u>ate</u> his lunch and most of mine.

eight means a number.

There are <u>eight</u> people in my family.

aye means yes. Everyone voted by saying, "<u>Aye</u>."

eye means used for seeing.

Brittany has a sty in her <u>eye</u>.

I is a pronoun. <u>I</u> like to write stories.

ball means a round object.

Milton caught every <u>ball</u>.

bawl means to cry.

The baby looks like she's going to <u>bawl</u>.

b

bare means not covered. My dad's head is <u>bare</u>.

bear means an animal. The <u>bear</u> growled at us.

be means to be alive.

Jacquie will <u>be</u> here any minute.

bee means an insect.

We stood still when

we saw the <u>bee</u>.

beach means the edge of a lake or sea.

My family's going to the <u>beach</u>.

beech means a kind of tree.

I think that's a <u>beech</u> tree.

beat means to whip. My team <u>beat</u> all the others.

beet means a red vegetable.

Mom sliced a <u>beet</u> for the salad.

berry means a kind of fruit. There's only one kind of <u>berry</u> in the salad.

bury means to cover up. My dog likes to <u>bury</u> things.

billed means charged. We were <u>billed</u> for someone else's phone calls.

build means put together. We plan to <u>build</u> some bookshelves in my room.

blew means did blow. The wind <u>blew</u> sand in our faces.

blue means a color. Corinne wore a <u>blue</u> shirt.

board means sawed wood. This <u>board</u> will work as a shelf for books.

bored means not interested. Phyllis says she's never <u>bored</u>.

b

brake means a part used for stopping.
Mom slammed her foot on the <u>brake</u>.

break means to come apart. I hope we
didn't <u>break</u> the window!

buy means to purchase.
Natalie needs to <u>buy</u> some pens.

by means near. We drove <u>by</u> the radio station.

cent means a penny.
I don't have a <u>cent</u> to my name!

sent means being asked to go.
Mom <u>sent</u> me to my room.

scent means an odor.
My dog is tracking some animal's <u>scent</u>.

cheap means of little cost.
I bought a <u>cheap</u> pair of boots.

cheep means a bird sound.
It sounded like a baby bird's <u>cheep</u>.

d

chews means to use teeth.

Meg's sister <u>chews</u> her nails.

choose means to select.

You may <u>choose</u> whichever one you'd like.

close means to shut. I have to remember to <u>close</u> the hamster's cage.

clothes means clothing.

We went shopping for school <u>clothes</u>.

creak means a noise.

I heard a scary <u>creak</u> in the night.

creek means a small stream. Let's wade across the <u>creek</u>.

deer means an animal.

A <u>deer</u> leaped across the road.

dear means much loved.

My grandma says I am <u>dear</u>.

d

desert means to go away from.

I promise I won't <u>desert</u> you.

dessert means part of a meal.

We had bread pudding for <u>dessert</u>.

die means to stop living.

I don't ever want my pets to <u>die</u>.

dye means to add color.

The red <u>dye</u> turned everything pink!

doe means a female deer. The fawn followed the <u>doe</u> into the stream.

dough means an unbaked mixture.

Cookie <u>dough</u> tastes good.

do means to work at. I will <u>do</u> that for you.

dew means water droplets.

<u>Dew</u> covered the ground this morning.

due means owed. My library book is <u>due</u> tomorrow.

f

fair means honest or just. It wasn't <u>fair</u>!

fare means cost. Do you need the exact <u>fare</u> to ride the subway?

find means uncover.
Could you help me <u>find</u> my jacket?

fined means charged.
I'll get <u>fined</u> if I've lost that book.

fir means a kind of tree. The snow-covered <u>fir</u> trees looked like ghosts.

fur means an animal's coat.
Some animals shed <u>fur</u> in the spring.

flea means an insect. I found a <u>flea</u> in the carpet.

flee means to run away.
Barkley tries to <u>flee</u> when I brush him.

f

flew means went away.

The birds <u>flew</u> off when I went outside.

flu means an illness. Fever and aching all over are

<u>flu</u> symptoms.

flour means ground grain.

My mom makes gravy with <u>flour</u>.

flower means a part of a plant.

A wild <u>flower</u> grew in the sidewalk crack.

for means the purpose of. I have news <u>for</u> you.

four means a number.

All <u>four</u> puppies curled up to sleep.

forth means forward.

We'll go <u>forth</u> when you're ready.

fourth means after third. Eddie is <u>fourth</u> in line.

h

gnu means an antelope.

The <u>gnu</u> looks much like an ox.

new means not old.

Our <u>new</u> sofa arrived last night.

knew means did know.

I <u>knew</u> you would understand.

grown means to get bigger.

I have <u>grown</u> three inches this year.

groan means a sound.

Don't <u>groan</u> when I tell you this.

guessed means decided without facts.

Tad says he <u>guessed</u> the answer.

guest means a visitor.

Our class is having a <u>guest</u> tomorrow.

hair means a head covering.

My <u>hair</u> is long and curly.

hare means a rabbit. We had a pet <u>hare</u> once.

h

hall means a passageway.

Ms. Tilly is coming down the <u>hall</u>.

haul means to carry.

Brenda has to <u>haul</u> all her books home.

hay means a dried grass.

We had to give <u>hay</u> to the horses.

hey means an expression. "<u>Hey</u>! Stop that!"

heal means to make well.

My broken arm will <u>heal</u> soon.

he'll means he will.

<u>He'll</u> never want to do this again!

heel means the back of the foot.

The shopping cart caught my <u>heel</u>.

hear means to use ears.

Timothea likes to <u>hear</u> scary stories.

here means this place. I can stay <u>here</u> with you.

h

heard means did hear. Pilar <u>heard</u> about it first.

herd means an animal group.
>   We ran down the hall
>   like a <u>herd</u> of buffaloes.

hi means a greeting. I said "<u>Hi</u>" to the new kid.

high means way up.
>   The temperature is too <u>high</u> in my room.

horse means an animal.
>   My best friend has her own <u>horse</u>.

hoarse means a husky voice.
>   I was <u>hoarse</u> after cheering at the game.

hole means an opening.
>   There's a <u>hole</u> in my favorite shirt.

whole means all. No one watched the <u>whole</u> movie.

k

knead means to mix with hands.

I will help you <u>knead</u> the yeast dough.

need means to want badly. Shelly may <u>need</u> some help too.

knight means a warrior.

My little brother loves to pretend he's a <u>knight</u>.

night means evening.

Our neighbor never goes out at <u>night</u>.

knot means a tied loop.

We need to tie a square <u>knot</u> here.

not means in no way. Arthur is <u>not</u> going with us.

know means to be sure of.

Do you <u>know</u> when the movie begins?

no means not so. There is <u>no</u> way that can be true!

m

made means created.

> A committee <u>made</u> costumes for the play.

maid means a hired person.

> My sister seems to think I am her <u>maid</u>.

mail means letters. I love to get <u>mail</u>.

male means a man. The paper said the <u>male</u> dancer stole the show.

main means important.

> Here's the <u>main</u> idea of the story.

mane means horse's hair. I got to comb Pauper's <u>mane</u> after the race.

Maine means a state.

> Augusta is the capital of <u>Maine</u>.

meat means animal flesh.

> Vegetarians prefer not to eat <u>meat</u>.

meet means to come together.

> Let's <u>meet</u> in the hall after school.

o

oar means a pole used to row.

Alex lost an <u>oar</u> in
the river.

or means you have a choice.

Do you want to see this movie <u>or</u> that one?

ore means a mineral. They hauled iron <u>ore</u> out of
the canyon.

one means a number.

Priscilla answered <u>one</u> question.

won means succeeded.

The Sox <u>won</u> the game last night.

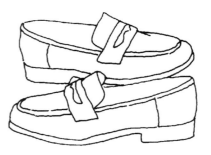

pair means two alike. Dominie has
a new <u>pair</u> of loafers.

pare means to peel.

I'd like it if you would <u>pare</u> this apple.

pear means a fruit.

That <u>pear</u> is bruised.

passed means moved beyond.

  You <u>passed</u> my house on your way home.

past means an earlier time.

  It's already <u>past</u> nine o'clock.

peace means a quiet time.

  Let's try for some <u>peace</u> in here.

piece means a part. May I have a <u>piece</u> of gum?

peak means the top of.

  I can hike to the <u>peak</u> of that mountain.

peek means to sneak a look.

  Don't you dare <u>peek</u> in that box!

pore means a skin gland.

  The doctor says it's a clogged <u>pore</u>.

pour means to flow out of.

  You may <u>pour</u> juice for all of us.

r

rain means wet weather. It will surely <u>rain</u> today.

rein means part of a horse's bridle.
Pull back on the <u>rein</u>.

read means to have gotten
meaning from print.
I <u>read</u> the best book!

red means a color.
Our school color is <u>red</u>.

real means not pretend.
Nonfiction is about <u>real</u> things.

reel means a part of a fishing pole.
Dad bought a new <u>reel</u> for his pole.

right means correct.
It may not seem <u>right</u>, but it's the rule.

write means to form letters.
Don't forget to <u>write</u>
me when you move.

ring means jewelry worn on a finger.
Demetrius lost his class <u>ring</u>.

wring means to squeeze.
<u>Wring</u> the rug to get the water out.

road means a street. That <u>road</u> goes nowhere.

rode means moved along on.
Tom and Adrian <u>rode</u> their bikes.

rowed means used oars.
Olivia said they <u>rowed</u> for hours.

rose means a flower. The <u>rose</u>bush is prickly.

rows means in lines. We'll have to line up in <u>rows</u>.

sail means to go by boat.
My grandparents will <u>sail</u>
to the Bahamas.

sale means lowered prices.
We found a fantastic
<u>sale</u> on shoes.

S

scene means place and time.

They found a wig at the <u>scene</u>.

seen means viewed. I have <u>seen</u> every new movie.

sea means a body of water.

The <u>sea</u> is full of plants.

see means to use eyes. Did you <u>see</u> what happened?

seam means where joined.

The <u>seam</u> in my shirt needs mending.

seem means appear to be.

They didn't <u>seem</u> to notice anything.

sew means to stitch. We'll need to
<u>sew</u> costumes next week.

so means therefore. I have to unlock the
door <u>so</u> others can enter.

sow means to plant.
Mom helped us <u>sow</u> grass seed.

S

soar means to fly high.

An eagle can <u>soar</u> a long time.

sore means painful. I have a <u>sore</u> throat.

some means an amount. You might bring along <u>some</u> of your music.

sum means the total when adding.

The <u>sum</u> is less than one hundred.

son means a boy or man. My aunt has a new <u>son</u>.

sun means a hot star.

The <u>sun</u> hid behind the billowy clouds.

stair means a step.

I thought I left my books on the <u>stair</u>.

stare means to look at. Everyone will <u>stare</u> at me!

t

tale means a story. Sheila told a scary <u>tale</u>.

tail means a body part. He'll wag his <u>tail</u> as soon as
he sees you.

their means there is ownership. The kids found
<u>their</u> own props for the play.

they're means they are. <u>They're</u> about to open
the curtain on Act I.

there means that place. If you put it <u>there</u>,
it should be easy to find.

theirs means there is ownership. He and his friends
think the room is <u>theirs.</u>

there's means there is.
<u>There's</u> a reason why we did it this way.

threw means having tossed. Who <u>threw</u>
this shirt in the laundry?

through means by way of.
Po came <u>through</u> the back door.

w

to means toward. Annette went <u>to</u> get more paper.

two means a number. <u>Two</u> heads are sometimes better than one.

too means also. I'd like to have one of those, <u>too</u>.

toad means an animal. I saw a <u>toad</u> on the sidewalk.

towed means pulled. Our van had to be <u>towed</u>.

toe means a part of the foot. Don't stub your <u>toe</u> on that brick.

tow means to pull. Who will <u>tow</u> the wrecked car?

waist means a body part just above the hips. My jeans are tight at the <u>waist</u>.

waste means to destroy. You'll <u>waste</u> time if you don't begin now.

w

wait means to stop a while.

Please <u>wait</u> for me outside.

weight means heaviness.

There's too much <u>weight</u> on one end.

weak means not strong.

Your argument is <u>weak</u>.

week means seven days.

Cecil had no homework
at all last <u>week</u>.

who's means who is. <u>Who's</u> going to go first?

whose means there is ownership.

<u>Whose</u> shoes are these?

wood means a product from a tree.

This <u>wood</u> box
is full.

would means willing to.

<u>Would</u> you like to tell us what you think?

Stuck with Each Other

(Compound Words)

groundhog

The two words <u>ground</u> and <u>hog</u> are "glued" together to make one word. One word made from two smaller words is a <u>compound word</u>.

What happens to the meanings of the little words? Sometimes the meanings change. For example, <u>understand</u> is a compound word. The little words <u>under</u> and <u>stand</u> are put together. But <u>understand</u> does not mean to stand under something! And a <u>brainstorm</u> is a good idea—it is not really a storm inside of the brain!

Here are some more compound words. The words are organized into categories. Can you think of more compound words?

Animals

anthill
bluebird
butterfly
catfish
dragonfly
earthworm
goldfish
jellyfish
longhorn
rattlesnake
wildcat
woodpecker

Body

armpit
eyelid
toenail
windpipe

Business

drugstore
junkyard
lumberyard
supermarket

Celebrations

birthday
Thanksgiving

Clothing

cutoffs
earring
nightgown
sweatshirt
turtleneck
underwear

Communication

goodbye
network
password
postcard
understand
videocassette

Descriptive Words

awesome
nationwide
oddball
outstanding
trustworthy
waterproof

Foods

applesauce
blueberry
breakfast
buttermilk
doughnut
gingerbread
grapefruit
gumball
meatball
mushroom
peanut
popcorn
strawberry
watermelon

Home

bathroom
bookshelf
carport
cupboard
doorbell

driveway
fireplace
rooftop
teapot
wallpaper

Music

bagpipe
earphones

Nature

buttercup
cattail
earthquake
iceberg
moonlight
quicksand
rainbow
seashell
snowstorm
sunflower
sunshine

Objects

billfold
candlestick
flashlight
handcuff
haystack
padlock
ponytail
something
suitcase
toothpaste
washcloth
wastebasket
yardstick

People

anybody
everyone
gentlemen
grandchild
nickname
sweetheart

Places

airport
anywhere
downstairs
fairgrounds
inside
lighthouse
offstage
outdoors
somewhere
treehouse
uptown

School

blackboard
classmate
homework
knapsack
notebook
playground

Sports & Recreation

baseball
basketball
dugout
hopscotch
joystick
kickball
playoffs
quarterback

sandbox
scoreboard
touchdown

Time

afternoon
daytime
meanwhile
midnight
weekend

Tools

jigsaw
sandpaper
sawhorse
screwdriver
stepladder

Transportation

airplane

freeway

handlebar

headlight

highway

motorcycle

railroad

rowboat

wheelchair

Work

cabinetmaker

cowboy

firefighter

landlord

lawmaker

lifeguard

ringmaster

Other Words

another

goosebump

itself

nightmare

runaway

tablespoon

whirlpool

Trade-Offs

(Contractions)

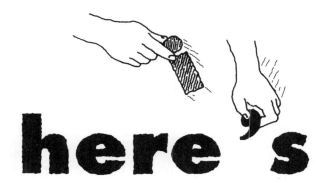

Some words are made by joining parts of two words. A <u>contraction</u> always has an apostrophe. Missing letters are traded for an apostrophe.

Here are some contractions you use when you speak. You may want to use contractions when you write a note or a letter to a friend.

he ~~has~~	he's	they ~~are~~	they're
he ~~is~~	he's	we ~~are~~	we're
here ~~is~~	here's	you ~~are~~	you're
I ~~am~~	I'm	what ~~is~~	what's
it ~~has~~	it's	I ~~would~~	I'd
it ~~is~~	it's	you ~~would~~	you'd
she ~~has~~	she's	I ~~have~~	I've
she ~~is~~	she's	we ~~have~~	we've
that ~~is~~	that's	I ~~will~~	I'll

you ~~will~~	you'll	is n~~o~~t	isn't
who ~~will~~	who'll	would n~~o~~t	wouldn't
let ~~us~~	let's	are n~~o~~t	aren't
can ~~not~~	can't	did n~~o~~t	didn't
do n~~o~~t	don't		

Can you add more contractions to the list?

_____   _____

_____   _____

_____   _____

___ _____   _____

Word Play

**(Onomatopoeia,
Palindromes,
Hink-Pinks,
Hinky-Pinkys)**

WHACK!

Writers work with words. Writers also play with words. You can have fun with the sounds of words. You can put words next to each other to say funny or odd things. You can turn a word's letters around to make a different word. You can even make up or "coin" new words whenever you want.

Here are some lists of Sound Words, Palindromes, Hink-Pinks, and Hinky-Pinkys. You may just want to play with these words and their sounds. Or you may want to use some of these fun words in your writing.

Onomatopoeia
(Sound Words)

Listen! What sounds do you hear around you? Sound words, or <u>onomatopoeia</u>, are words that spell actual sounds.

Sometimes every letter of a sound word is written in capital letters.

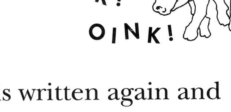

OINK!

Sometimes a sound word is written again and again.

DRIP! DRIP! DRIP!

Sometimes the first or last letter of a sound word is repeated:

r-r-ring   who-o-o-o

And sometimes the letters of a sound word are stretched out:

C R E A K!

Here are some more words for sounds. The words are organized under some general categories. Can you think of more sound words?

Animal Sounds

baa

buzz

cheep

chirp

clip-clop

cluck

cock-a-doodle-do

cuckoo

growl

hiss

meow

moo

neigh

purr

quack

squeak

tweet

woof

Bumping/ Falling Sounds

bang

clang

crash

kerplop

ping

plop

scrunch

smack

splash

splat

thump

whack

zing

zonk

People Sounds

giggle

ha-ha

hmmm

kerchoo

oomph

ugh

waa

yuck

CRASH!

119

Machine Sounds	Weather Sounds	Other Sound Words
beep	bang	bubble
boing	boom	crinkle
choo-choo	crash	fizz
clank	ping	glug
click	zing	gurgle
ding-dong		sizzle
ping		slurp
pop		swish
squeak		whoosh
tick-tock		zap
whirr		zip
zoom		zoom

s i z z l e

Palindromes

Can you tell which chick is saying "peep"? Is it the chick on the left? or the chick on the right?

p e e p

It doesn't matter, does it? The word PEEP is spelled the same way backward and forward! The word PEEP is a <u>palindrome</u>.

Here are some more words that are spelled the same way backward and forward. Can you think of other palindromes?

Anna	gag	sees
bob	kayak	toot
dad	mom	tot
did	noon	
eye	pop	

Some words can be arranged so that a sentence is a palindrome. Check out these palindrome sentences. Do they read the same way backward and forward? Can you make up some more palindrome sentences?

Now Dad won. _____

Ward did draw. _____

We sew. _____

Hink-Pinks

hay play

The two words <u>hay</u> and <u>play</u> rhyme. <u>Hay</u> is a one-syllable word, and <u>play</u> is a one-syllable word.

A <u>hink-pink</u> is two one-syllable words that rhyme. Here are some more hink-pinks. Can you make up others?

ham jam

mad dad

leaf thief

mice rice

Hinky-Pinkys

The words <u>Humpty</u> and <u>Dumpty</u> rhyme. <u>Humpty</u> is a two-syllable word, and <u>Dumpty</u> is a two-syllable word.

A <u>hinky-pinky</u> is two two-syllable words that rhyme. Here are some more hinky-pinkys. Can you make up others?

hokey-pokey

muscle tussle

walkie-talkie

See if you can find more hink-pinks and hinky-pinkys in the rhyming word lists that begin on page 132 of this book.

Rhyme Time

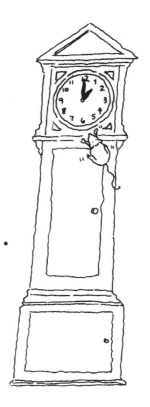

**Hickory dickory dock
The mouse ran up the clock . . .**

What is a rhyming sound?

Two words that rhyme have the same ending sound. Their ending sound is called a <u>rhyming sound</u>.

Rhyming sounds are all around you. You hear rhyming sounds in nursery rhymes. You also hear rhyming sounds in poems and songs and jump-rope jingles.

A rhyming sound always begins with a vowel. A rhyming sound can be written by writing the alphabet letter or letters that you hear in that sound. For example, the rhyming sound at the

**Jack and Jill
went up the hill . . .**

**Jack Sprat
could eat no fat . . .**

ends of the words <u>dock</u> and <u>clock</u> can be written <u>ok</u>. The rhyming sound in <u>Jill</u> and <u>hill</u> can be written <u>il</u>. And the rhyming sound in <u>Sprat</u> and <u>fat</u> can be written <u>at</u>.

What is a rhyming-word family? Rhyming words can be grouped into families—just like people! In a rhyming-word family, every word has the same ending sound.

Here are two families of rhyming words. One family includes words that end in the <u>at</u> sound. So we might call that family the "<u>at</u> as in <u>fat</u>" family. The other family of words might be called the "<u>ath</u> as in <u>math</u>" family.

at as in *fat*

at
bat
brat
cat
chat
fat
flat
gnat
hat
mat
pat
rat
sat
that

ath as in *math*

bath
math
path

Some human families have many people in them. And some human families are small, with only two or three people. Like human families, rhyming-word families may be large or small. Some rhyming-word families have many words in them. Others have few.

How do I find words that rhyme? More than 200 rhyming-word families are listed on the following pages. So how will you find any one family of rhyming words? Let's find out!

Suppose you want to find the family of words that rhyme with the word <u>toes</u>. To find the words that rhyme with <u>toes</u>, you'll need to know the ending sound in the word. Then you'll need to know which alphabet letters could spell that sound. So you'll need to answer two questions:

Question #1: What is the ending sound in the word <u>toes</u>?

Your Answer: I hear the sound of long <u>o</u> and the sound that the letter <u>z</u> makes.

Question #2: What alphabet letter or letters could spell that ending sound?

Your Answer: The letters <u>oz</u> could spell that sound.

Now you're ready to look for <u>oz</u> in the lists of rhyming words on the following pages. The families of rhyming words are listed in alphabetical order under the vowels A, E, I, O, and U. Remember, a rhyming sound always begins with a vowel. So the family of <u>oz</u> words will be found under the vowel **O**.

Turn to page 163 in this book. Look for the large vowel letter **O**. Look down the lists of words under the large vowel **O**. You will find <u>oz</u> as in <u>nose</u> on page 177. Do the words <u>toes</u> and <u>nose</u> rhyme? Yes! All the words in the <u>oz</u> as in <u>nose</u> family rhyme with the word <u>toes</u>.

Wow! Look at all those words that rhyme with the word <u>toes</u>. Count them . . . twenty-two words! What a large family!

toes   **crows**   **bows**

And guess what! There are even more words that rhyme with the word <u>toes</u>. You may want to add other words, like <u>throws</u> or a girl's name <u>Rose</u>.

Sometimes the ending sound you hear in a word can be written different ways. For example, the ending sound you hear in the word <u>moose</u> might be written <u>us</u> or <u>oos</u>. So you will find words that rhyme with the word <u>moose</u> listed under the vowel **O** (<u>oos</u> as in <u>moose</u>) and under the vowel **U** (<u>us</u> as in <u>moose</u>).

Now and then, you may find a word that doesn't seem to rhyme with the other words in a family. That's because different people say some words in different ways.

Remember: any time you have a word and want to find its family of rhyming words, you begin by asking (and answering!) two questions:

1. What is the ending sound in your word?

2. What alphabet letters could spell that ending sound?

Then you can use the list of rhyming-word families to find just what you want!

What is a STEP AHEAD list of words?

The word <u>nose</u> has one syllable. And so do the first twenty-two words in the family of words that rhyme with the word <u>nose</u>.**

So what are those other eight words, like <u>borrows</u> and <u>heroes</u> and <u>windows</u>? Those longer words also rhyme with the words <u>nose</u> and <u>toes</u>. But when you say one of those longer words, you don't hear just one syllable. You hear two syllables!

**A pair of one-syllable words that rhyme can suggest a funny or interesting idea that's called a <u>hink-pink</u>. Look for <u>leaf thief</u>, <u>snake shake</u>, and other hink-pinks as you use the lists of rhyming-word families.

Sometimes when you are writing, you may want to use a longer word that rhymes with a short word. That's when you will want to use one of the **STEP AHEAD** lists of two-syllable words.

To see the names of all the families of rhyming words included in this book, look for the <u>Index of Rhyming-Word Families</u> on page 195 at the back of this book.

Rhyming-Word Families

A

a as in *day*

bay
clay
day
gray
hay
hey
Jay
lay
May
neigh
pay
play
pray
Ray
say
sleigh

spray
stay
they
tray
way
weigh

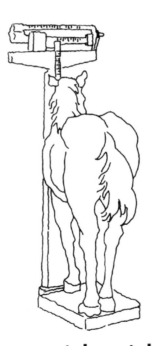

neigh weigh

STEP AHEAD

away
ballet
birthday
bouquet
delay
display
halfway
hallway
highway
hooray
okay
relay
runway
subway
Sunday
today
x-ray

a as in *raw*

ah

caw

claw

draw

gnaw

ha

jaw

law

ma

pa

paw

raw

saw

slaw

squaw

straw

thaw

STEP AHEAD

coleslaw

grandma

grandpa

hurrah

jigsaw

seesaw

Utah

crab gab

ab as in *cab*

blab

cab

crab

dab

drab

gab

grab

lab

nab

scab

slab

stab

tab

ach as in *catch*

batch

catch

hatch

latch

match

patch

scratch

snatch

a

ad as in *made*

aid
blade
braid
fade
grade
made
maid
paid
played
prayed
raid
shade
stayed
trade
wade
weighed

mad dad

STEP AHEAD

afraid
arcade
Band-aid
bridesmaid
delayed
displayed
homemade
invade
lampshade
mermaid
parade
stockade

ad as in *dad*

add
bad
Chad
dad
fad
glad
had
lad
mad
pad
sad

aft as in *raft*

craft
draft
graphed
laughed
raft
shaft

ag as in *wag*

bag

brag

drag

flag

gag

nag

rag

sag

snag

tag

wag

aj as in *page*

age

cage

gauge

page

rage

stage

wage

ak as in *make*

bake

brake

break

cake

fake

flake

Jake

lake

make

quake

rake

shake

snake

steak

take

wake

STEP AHEAD

awake

cupcake

earthquake

headache

keepsake

mistake

pancake

snowflake

toothache

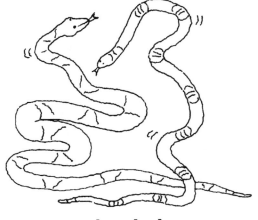

snake shake

a

ak as in *pack*

back
black
crack
jack
pack
quack
rack
sack
shack
smack
snack
stack
track
yak

aks as in *tax*

acts
ax
cracks
facts
fax
jacks
packs
sacks
smacks
stacks
tax
tracks
wax

akt as in *fact*

act
backed
cracked
fact
packed
sacked
tracked

STEP AHEAD

attract
contact
contract
exact
react
subtract

yak pack

al as in *pal*

Al
gal
pal
shall

al as in *fall*

all
ball
call
crawl
doll
fall
hall
mall
Paul
small
stall
tall
wall

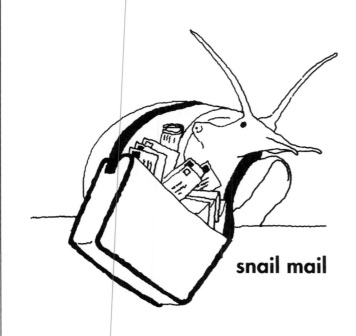

snail mail

al as in *sale*

bale
Braille
fail
hail
jail
mail
male
nail
pail
quail

rail
sail
sale
scale
snail
tail
tale
they'll
trail
whale

a

am as in *game*	**am** as in *jam*	**amp** as in *lamp*
aim	am	camp
blame	clam	champ
came	ham	clamp
claim	jam	cramp
fame	lamb	damp
flame	ram	lamp
frame	Sam	ramp
game	scram	stamp
name	slam	tramp
same	swam	
shame	wham	
tame	yam	

tame flame

brain drain

pain
plain
plane
rain
rein
sane
slain
Spain
sprain
stain
train
vane
vein
Wayne

an as in *cane*

brain
cane
chain
crane
drain
gain
grain
lane
main
Maine
mane

an as in *can*

an
can
fan
man
pan
plan
ran
Stan
tan
than
van

STEP AHEAD

airplane
contain
explain
remain

STEP AHEAD

began
Japan
pecan
suntan

a

and as in *hand*

and
band
brand
canned
fanned
gland
grand
hand
land
planned
sand
stand

ants dance

ang as in *rang*

bang
clang
fang
gang
rang
sang

ank as in *tank*

bank
blank
drank
Hank
prank
sank
spank
tank
thank

ans as in *dance*

ants
chance
chants
dance
France
glance
pants
plants

ant as in *paint*

faint
paint
saint

ant as in *can't*

ant
aunt
can't
chant
grant
plant

STEP AHEAD

command
demand
expand
quicksand

ap as in *tape*

ape
cape
drape
grape
scrape
shape
tape

ap as in *map*

cap
clap
flap
gap
lap
map
nap
scrap
slap
snap
strap
tap

trap
wrap

ar as in *hair*

air
bare
bear
care
chair
dare
fair
fare
glare
hair
hare
pair
pear

bear chair

prayer
rare
scare
share
spare
square
stair
stare
swear
tear
their
there
they're
wear
where

STEP AHEAD

beware
compare
prepare
repair
unfair

a

ar as in *car*

are
bar
car
far
jar
scar
star
tar

ard as in *yard*

barred
card
guard
hard
lard
scarred
yard

ark as in *park*

ark
bark
dark
mark
park
shark
spark

STEP AHEAD

boxcar
guitar
jaguar
streetcar

STEP AHEAD

barnyard
graveyard
leotard
lifeguard
postcard

STEP AHEAD

aardvark
birthmark
bookmark

arm as in *farm*

arm
charm
farm
harm

bark park

heart part

art as in *cart*

art

cart

chart

dart

heart

part

smart

start

as as in *base*

ace

base

brace

case

chase

face

Grace

lace

place

race

space

trace

vase

STEP AHEAD

erase

shoelace

staircase

suitcase

---

as as in *gas*

brass

class

gas

glass

grass

pass

ash as in *dash*

cash

clash

crash

dash

flash

rash

slash

smash

splash

trash

ask as in *mask*

ask

cask

mask

task

a

ast as in *paste*

based
baste
chased
faced
paste
placed
spaced
taste
traced
waist
waste

ast as in *last*

blast
cast
fast
last
passed
past

at as in *gate*

ate
bait
date
eight
gate
great
hate
late
plate
skate
state
straight
strait
wait
weight

STEP AHEAD

classmate
create
donate
locate
playmate

The great plate wait.

a

cat chat

az as in *days*

days
lays
maize
maze
neighs
pays
plays
praise
prays
sprays
stays
vase
ways
weighs

at as in *fat*

at
bat
brat
cat
chat
fat
flat
gnat
hat
mat
pat
rat
sat
that

ath as in *math*

bath
math
path

av as in *gave*

brave
cave
gave
grave
save
shave
slave
they've
wave

az as in *jazz*

as
has
jazz

E

e as in *fee*

be
bee
flea
free
he
key
knee
me
pea
sea

see
she
ski
tea
three
tree
we
wee

STEP AHEAD

agree
easy
monkey
teepee
trophy

Said the flea to the bee,
"It's a mystery to me
how, with wings that are wee,
you can fly so easily."

Said the bee to the flea,
"I'm no curiosity!
Though my wings may be wee,
they are perfect for a bee."

ech as in *teach*

beach
bleach
each
peach
reach
speech
teach

ed as in *bead*

bead
bleed
breed
feed
knead
lead
need
read
seed
skied
speed
we'd
weed

e

ed as in *head*

bed
bread
dead
fed
head
lead
led
read
red
said
sled
spread
thread
wed

leaf thief

ef as in *beef*

beef
brief
chief
grief
leaf
thief

ef as in *deaf*

chef
deaf
Jeff

STEP AHEAD

ahead
bedspread
bunkbed
forehead
instead

eg as in *leg*

beg
egg
Greg
leg
Peg

ek as in *week*

beak
cheek
creek
leak
peek
sneak
speak
squeak
weak
week

e

ek as in *neck*

check
deck
neck
peck
wreck

el as in *heal*

deal
eel
feel
he'll
heal
heel
kneel
meal
peel
real
seal
she'll
squeal
steal

steel
we'll
wheel

swell smell

el as in *fell*

bell
cell
fell
sell
shell
smell
spell
swell
tell
well
yell

eld as in *yelled*

held
smelled
spelled
weld
yelled

elf as in *self*

elf
self
shelf

STEP AHEAD

bookshelf
herself
himself
itself
myself
yourself

elt as in *melt*

belt
felt
melt
pelt
smelt

em as in *seam*

beam
cream
dream
scream
seam
seem
steam
stream
team

em as in *hem*

gem
hem
M
stem
them

en as in *mean*

bean
clean
Dean
Gene
green
mean
queen
screen
seen

en as in *pen*

den
hen
men
N
pen
ten
then
when
wren

end as in *send*

bend
blend
end
friend
lend
mend
send
spend

dream team

e

ens as in *fence*

cents
fence
scents
sense
tents

ent as in *tent*

bent
cent
dent
meant
rent
scent
sent
spent
tent
went

ep as in *keep*

beep
cheap
creep
deep
heap
jeep
keep
leap
peep
sheep
sleep
steep
sweep
weep

er as in *dear*

cheer
clear
dear
deer
ear
fear
gear
hear
here
near
pier
rear
sheer
smear
spear
steer
tear
year

sheep leap

e

geese peace

es as in *geese*

cease

crease

fleece

geese

grease

lease

niece

peace

piece

guess

less

mess

press

stress

yes

es as in *guess*

bless

chess

dress

est as in *feast*

beast

ceased

east

feast

least

yeast

est as in *test*

best

blest

breast

chest

dressed

guessed

guest

nest

pest

quest

rest

stressed

test

vest

west

e

et as in *feet*

beat

beet

cheat

eat

feet

greet

heat

meat

meet

neat

seat

sheet

sleet

street

suite

sweet

treat

wheat

pet

set

sweat

threat

vet

wet

yet

wet pet

et as in *jet*

bet

debt

get

jet

let

met

net

ex as in *necks*

checks

decks

necks

pecks

wrecks

i

ez as in *keys*

breeze

cheese

ease

fees

fleas

freeze

he's

keys

knees

peas

please

seas

she's

skis

sneeze

squeeze

tease

these

trees

I

i as in *pie*

buy

by

bye

cry

die

dry

dye

eye

fly

fry

guy

hi

high

I

lie

lye

my

pie

shy

sigh

sky

spy

thigh

tie

try

why

ib as in *rib*

bib

crib

fib

rib

high fly

i

ich as in *rich*

ditch
hitch
itch
pitch
rich
stitch
switch
which
witch

id as in *ride*

bride
cried
died
dried
fried
guide
hide
I'd
lied
ride
side
sighed
slide
spied
tide
tried
wide

STEP AHEAD

beside
decide
divide
inside
outside

id as in *did*

bid
did
hid
kid
lid
rid

skid
slid
squid

if as in *life*

knife
life
wife

ift as in *gift*

drift
gift
lift
shift
sift
sniffed
swift
thrift

bride ride

i

pig jig

ig as in *fig*

big

dig

fig

jig

pig

sprig

swig

twig

wig

ik as in *like*

bike

dike

hike

like

spike

strike

ik as in *lick*

brick

chick

click

kick

lick

Nick

pick

quick

sick

slick

stick

thick

tick

trick

STEP AHEAD

attic

chopstick

homesick

magic

picnic

plastic

toothpick

i

iks as in *fix*

bricks
chicks
clicks
fix
kicks
licks
mix
picks
six
sticks
ticks
tricks

STEP AHEAD

attics
chopsticks
picnics
toothpicks

il as in *mile*

dial
file
I'll
mile
pile
smile
tile
while

il as in *hill*

bill
chill
dill
drill
fill
gill
grill
hill
ill
kill
mill

pill
skill
spill
still
thrill
till
will

ild as in *wild*

child
dialed
filed
mild
piled
smiled
wild

hill spill

ild as in *filled*

billed
build
chilled
drilled
filled
grilled
killed
skilled
spilled
thrilled

im as in *dime*

chime
climb
crime
dime
I'm
rhyme
time

STEP AHEAD

bedtime
daytime
mealtime
meantime
springtime

im as in *him*

dim
grim
gym
him
Kim
limb
rim
slim
swim
Tim
trim

in as in *line*

dine
fine
line
mine
nine
pine
shine
sign
spine
vine
whine

Gym & Swim

i

in as in **pin**	**ind** as in **kind**	**ing** as in **sing**
bin	blind	bring
chin	dined	cling
fin	find	king
grin	fined	ping
in	grind	ring
inn	kind	sing
pin	lined	sling
shin	mind	spring
sin	shined	sting
skin	signed	string
spin	whined	swing
thin		thing
tin	**ind** as in **pinned**	wing
twin		
win	chinned	
	grinned	
	pinned	
	sinned	
	skinned	
	spinned	

spring thing

i

ink as in *sink*

blink

drink

ink

link

mink

pink

rink

shrink

sink

slink

stink

think

wink

inks as in *winks*

blinks

drinks

jinx

links

lynx

rinks

shrinks

sinks

slinks

sphinx

stinks

thinks

winks

ins as in *since*

hints

mints

prince

prints

rinse

since

splints

sprints

squints

tints

int as in *mint*

hint

lint

mint

print

splint

sprint

squint

tint

prince rinse

i

ip as in *ripe*

gripe
pipe
ripe
stripe
swipe
type
wipe

ip as in *dip*

chip
clip
dip
drip
flip
grip
hip
lip

rip
ship
sip
skip
slip
snip
strip
tip
trip
whip
zip

ir as in *tire*

fire
hire
tire
wire

mice rice

is as in *rice*

dice
ice
lice
mice
nice
price
rice
slice
spice
twice

is as in *miss*

hiss
kiss
miss
sis
this

i

ish as in *wish*

dish
fish
squish
swish
wish

fish dish

ist as in *list*

fist
hissed
kissed
list
missed
mist
twist

it as in *kite*

bite
bright
fight
flight
fright
height
kite
knight
light
might
night
quite
right
sight
tight
white
write

knight fright

it as in *sit*

bit
fit

hit
it
kit
knit
lit
mitt
pit
quit
sit
skit
slit
spit
split
wit

i

iv as in *five*

dive

drive

five

hive

I've

jive

iz as in *pies*

buys

cries

dies

dries

eyes

flies

fries

guys

lies

pies

prize

rise

sighs

size

skies

spies

thighs

ties

tries

wise

iz as in *his*

fizz

his

is

Ms.

quiz

whiz

prize pies

no dough

o as in *go*

blow
bow
crow
doe
dough
flow
glow

go
grow
hoe
know
low
mow
no
oh
owe
pro
row
sew
show
slow
snow
so
sow
throw
toe
tow

STEP AHEAD

ago
although
below
borrow
burro
elbow
hello
hero
pillow
rainbow
shadow
window

o

ob as in *job*

Bob
cob
glob
job
knob
mob
rob
slob
snob
sob
throb

od as in *road*

bowed
code
crowed
flowed
glowed
hoed
load
mowed

owed
road
rode
rowed
sewed
showed
slowed
snowed
sowed
toad
towed

og as in *fog*

clog
dog
fog
frog
hog
jog
log

oi as in *toy*

boy
Joy
soy
toy
Troy

STEP AHEAD

annoy
cowboy
destroy
enjoy

log hog

oil as in *soil*

boil

broil

coil

foil

oil

soil

spoil

ois as in *voice*

choice

Joyce

Royce

voice

oiz as in *noise*

boys

joys

noise

poise

toys

ok as in *joke*

broke

choke

cloak

Coke

croak

joke

oak

poke

smoke

soak

spoke

stroke

woke

yoke

clock rock

ok as in *lock*

block

clock

crock

dock

flock

hawk

hock

knock

lock

pock

rock

shock

sock

wok

o

oks as in *fox*	**ol** as in *hole*	**ol** as in *fall*
blocks	bowl	all
box	coal	ball
clocks	goal	call
crocks	hole	crawl
docks	mole	doll
flocks	pole	fall
fox	roll	hall
knocks	scroll	mall
locks	soul	Paul
ox	stole	small
pox	toll	stall
rocks	whole	tall
shocks		wall
socks		

mole hole

old as in *fold*

bold
bowled
cold
fold
gold
hold
mold
old
rolled
sold
told

olk as in *walk*

chalk
stalk
talk
walk

om as in *home*

comb
dome
foam
home
roam

om as in *mom*

bomb
mom
prom
Tom

on as in *bone*

blown
bone
cone
flown
grown
known
loan
lone

phone zone

moan
own
phone
sewn
shone
shown
sown
stone
throne
thrown
tone
zone

STEP AHEAD

alone
backbone
headphone

167

o

dawn yawn

ong as in *long*

gong
long
song
wrong

STEP AHEAD

along
belong
Hong Kong
King Kong

on as in *lawn*

dawn
drawn
fawn
gone
lawn
on
swan
yawn

ond as in *bond*

blond
bond
dawned
fond
frond
pond
wand
yawned

oo as in *few*

cue
few
mew
pew
view
yew

oo as in *zoo*

blew
blue
boo
brew
chew
clue
crew
dew
do
drew
due
flew
glue
gnu
grew
knew
moo
new
shoe
stew
sue
through

to
too
true
two
who
you
zoo

STEP AHEAD

bamboo
cuckoo
into
kerchoo
shampoo
unto

ood as in *good*

could
good
hood
should
stood
wood
would

ood as in *mood*

chewed
dude
food
glued
mood
rude
stewed
you'd

**It's easy to see
this dude is a Rude–
He talks while his mouth
is crammed full of food.**

169

o

oof as in *roof*

goof

hoof

poof

proof

roof

woof

*If I don't know
on which page to look,
I'll use the index
in the back of the book.*

ook as in *cook*

book

cook

crook

hook

look

shook

took

ool as in *cool*

cool

cruel

drool

fool

pool

rule

school

spool

stool

tool

oom as in *room*

bloom

boom

broom

doom

gloom

groom

loom

room

tomb

whom

zoom

oon as in *moon*

dune

June

moon

noon

prune

soon

spoon

tune

STEP AHEAD

baboon

balloon

cartoon

cocoon

monsoon

raccoon

o

oop as in *soup*

coop

droop

group

hoop

loop

scoop

sloop

snoop

soup

stoop

swoop

oos as in *moose*

goose

juice

loose

moose

noose

spruce

truce

Zeus

Norman Newt can toot a flute.

oot as in *suit*

boot

chute

flute

fruit

hoot

loot

newt

root

route

scoot

shoot

suit

toot

ooth as in *tooth*

booth

Ruth

sleuth

tooth

truth

youth

oov as in *you've*

groove

move

prove

you've

STEP AHEAD

improve

remove

---

o

ooz as in *lose*

blues
boos
bruise
chews
choose
clues
crews
cruise
dues
fuse
glues
gnus
lose
shoes
snooze
stews
sues
use
whose

STEP AHEAD

abuse
accuse
amuse
confuse
cuckoos
excuse
refuse
shampoos
tissues

Dad was getting
bald on top,
but now he sports a
brand new mop.

op as in *soap*

hope
nope
rope
slope
soap

op as in *hop*

chop
cop
crop
drop
flop
hop
mop
pop
shop
stop
top

o

floor chore

score

shore

snore

sore

store

war

wore

your

or as in *pour*

bore

chore

door

drawer

floor

for

four

more

oar

or

poor

pour

roar

ord as in *roared*

board

bored

cord

lord

poured

roared

scored

snored

stored

sword

ward

orn as in *corn*

born

corn

horn

morn

thorn

torn

warn

worn

ors as in *horse*

coarse

course

force

horse

173

o

ort as in *fort*

court
fort
quart
short
sort
sport
wart

court sport

os as in *loss*

boss
cross
floss
loss
moss
sauce
toss

ost as in *most*

boast
coast
ghost
host
most
post
roast
toast

ost as in *cost*

bossed
cost
crossed
flossed
frost
lost
tossed

ghost host

ot as in *goat*

boat
coat
float
goat
note
oat
throat
tote
vote
wrote

ot as in *hot*

clot

cot

dot

got

hot

jot

knot

lot

not

plot

pot

rot

shot

slot

spot

squat

swat

taut

tot

trot

what

ot as in *taught*

bought

brought

caught

fought

sought

taught

thought

ow as in *cow*

bow

brow

chow

cow

how

now

plow

sow

wow

owch as in *pouch*

couch

grouch

ouch

pouch

owd as in *loud*

bowed

cloud

crowd

loud

plowed

proud

cloud crowd

o

own as in *down*	**ownd** as in *found*	**owr** as in *sour*
brown	bound	flour
clown	clowned	flower
crown	crowned	hour
down	drowned	our
drown	found	power
frown	frowned	shower
gown	ground	sour
noun	hound	tower
town	mound	
	pound	**ows** as in *house*
	round	blouse
	sound	house
	wound	louse
		mouse
		spouse

clown frown

o

owt as in *pout*

doubt
out
pout
scout
shout
snout
spout
sprout
trout

oz as in *nose*

blows
bows
chose
close
clothes
crows
flows
froze
glows
goes
grows
hoes
hose
nose
owes
pose
rows
shows
snows
those
toes
tows

STEP AHEAD

about
campout
cookout
lookout
without

STEP AHEAD

borrows
burros
elbows
heroes
pillows
rainbows
shadows
windows

Rose hoes rows

U

I poured it on and rubbed it through
before I read the label: GLUE!

two

who

woo

you

zoo

U

u as in *zoo*

blew

blue

boo

chew

clue

crew

dew

do

drew

due

flew

glue

gnu

grew

knew

moo

new

shoe

shoo

stew

sue

threw

through

to

too

true

STEP AHEAD

bamboo

cuckoo

into

kerchoo

shampoo

tissue

unto

u as in *few*

few

mew

pew

view

yew

ub as in *rub*

club
cub
hub
rub
scrub
shrub
stub
sub
tub

tub scrub

uch as in *such*

crutch
hutch
much
such
touch

ud as in *mood*

chewed
dude
food
glued
mood
rude
stewed
you'd

ud as in *mud*

blood
bud
flood
mud

udj as in *fudge*

budge
fudge
judge
smudge

uf as in *roof*

goof
hoof
poof
proof
roof
woof

uf as in *cuff*

bluff
buff
cuff
fluff
gruff
huff
muff
puff
rough
scuff
stuff
tough

U

ug as in *rug*

bug

chug

drug

dug

hug

jug

mug

plug

rug

shrug

slug

smug

snug

tug

snug bug

uk as in *duck*

buck

chuck

cluck

duck

luck

puck

struck

stuck

suck

truck

tuck

yuck

ul as in *cool*

cool

cruel

drool

fool

pool

rule

school

spool

stool

tool

ul as in *full*

bull

full

pull

wool

STEP AHEAD

bedbug

earplug

fireplug

humbug

bloom groom

um as in **room**

bloom
boom
broom
doom
gloom
groom
room
tomb
whom
zoom

um as in **gum**

bum
chum
come
crumb
drum
dumb
from
glum
gum
hum
mum
plum
scum
slum
some
strum
sum
thumb
yum

STEP AHEAD

become
eardrum
welcome

ump as in **jump**

bump
clump
dump
grump
hump
jump
lump
pump
slump
stump
thump

U

un as in *moon*

dune
June
moon
noon
prune
soon
spoon
tune

un as in *fun*

bun
done
fun
gun
hon
none
one
run
son
sun
ton
won

unch as in *lunch*

brunch
bunch
crunch
lunch

lunch bunch

munch
punch
scrunch

ung as in *young*

hung
lung
sprung
strung
stung
sung
tongue
young

STEP AHEAD

baboon
balloon
cartoon
cocoon
lagoon
monsoon
raccoon
teaspoon
typhoon

U

unk as in *junk*

bunk

chunk

clunk

drunk

dunk

flunk

junk

monk

shrunk

skunk

spunk

stunk

sunk

trunk

up as in *soup*

droop

group

hoop

loop

scoop

snoop

soup

troop

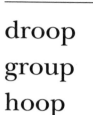

soup scoop

up as in *pup*

cup

pup

up

ur as in *fur*

blur

burr

cure

fir

fur

her

poor

pure

purr

sir

stir

sure

were

you're

your

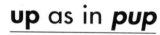

STEP AHEAD

hiccup

lineup

makeup

teacup

skunk stunk

183

U

urch as in *search*

birch
church
perch
search

bird word

urd as in *herd*

bird
blurred
curd
heard
herd
purred
stirred

third
word

urk as in *work*

clerk
jerk
perk
quirk
shirk
work

url as in *girl*

curl
earl
girl

pearl
squirrel
swirl
twirl
whirl

urld as in *world*

curled
swirled
twirled
whirled
world

urm as in *germ*

firm
germ
perm
squirm
term
worm

urn as in *learn*

burn
churn
earn
fern
learn
turn
urn

urs as in *verse*

curse
hearse
nurse
purse
verse
worse

urst as in *first*

burst
cursed
first

loose moose

nursed
thirst
worst

urt as in *dirt*

blurt
curt
dirt
flirt
hurt
shirt
skirt
spurt
squirt

us as in *moose*

goose
juice
loose
moose
noose
spruce
truce
Zeus

us as in *bus*

bus
cuss
fuss
muss
plus
pus
thus
us

U

ush as in *push*

bush
push
whoosh

flute toot

ush as in *rush*

blush
brush
crush
flush
hush
plush
rush
slush

usk as in *tusk*

dusk
husk
musk
tusk

ust as in *must*

bussed
bust
crust
dust
fussed
just
mussed
must
rust
thrust
trust

ut as in *suit*

boot
chute
flute
fruit
hoot
loot
newt
root
route
shoot
suit
toot

STEP AHEAD

compute
salute
uproot

ut as in *cut*

but
cut
hut
mutt
nut
putt
rut
shut
strut

STEP AHEAD

chestnut
doughnut
peanut
walnut

ut as in *put*

foot
put

**Whose shoes
are whose?**

uth as in *tooth*

booth
Ruth
tooth
truth
youth

uv as in *you've*

move
prove
you've

uv as in *love*

dove
glove
love
shove

uz as in *lose*

blues
boos
bruise
chews
choose
clues
dues
gnus
lose
shoes
snooze
stews
use
whose

uz as in *fuzz*

buzz
does
fuzz
was

Glossary

Index of
Rhyming-Word Families

Index of
Synonyms

Index

Glossary

Antonym

A word that means the opposite of another word.

Cliché

A figure of speech that is overused.

Compound word

A word made up of two or more smaller words.

Contraction

A short form of two words. An apostrophe is used in place of a missing letter or letters.

Dewey Decimal System

A system that organizes library books into ten main categories.

Ellipsis

Three periods used when one or more words have been left out.

f

Figurative language

Phrases whose meanings are different from their literal or real meanings.

Figure of speech

A phrase that has a meaning different from its literal or real meaning.

Formal writing

Writing, such as a business letter or manuscript, that is meant to be read by people other than oneself or friends.

Hink-pink

A pair of one-syllable rhyming words that suggest an interesting or funny idea.

Hinky-pinky

A pair of two-syllable rhyming words that suggest an interesting or funny idea.

Homograph

A word that is spelled like another word but has a different meaning and is sometimes pronounced differently.

Homophone

A word that sounds like another word but has a different spelling and different meaning.

Informal writing

Writing, such as notes or friendly letters, that is meant to be read by oneself or friends.

Library of Congress System

A system that organizes library books into main categories noted by a letter of the alphabet.

Metaphor

A figure of speech that compares two ideas.

One-syllable rhyme

One-syllable word endings that sound alike.

Onomatopoeia

A word, such as <u>woof</u>, whose pronunciation imitates a real sound.

p

Palindrome

A word, phrase, sentence, or number that reads the same way backward or forward.

Proofreader

A person who makes corrections to a piece of writing.

Rhyming sounds

Word endings that sound alike.

Rhyming word family

A group of words whose endings sound alike.

Simile

A figure of speech that uses the words <u>like</u> or <u>as</u> to compare two ideas.

Synonym

A word that means the same or nearly the same as another word.

Index of Rhyming-Word Families

a as in *day*
a as in *raw*
ab as in *cab*
ach as in *catch*
ad as in *made*
ad as in *dad*
aft as in *raft*
ag as in *wag*
aj as in *page*
ak as in *make*
ak as in *pack*
aks as in *tax*
akt as in *fact*
al as in *sale*
al as in *pal*
al as in *fall*
am as in *game*
am as in *jam*

amp as in *lamp*
an as in *cane*
an as in *can*
and as in *hand*
ang as in *rang*
ank as in *tank*
ans as in *dance*
ant as in *paint*
ant as in *can't*
ap as in *tape*
ap as in *map*
ar as in *hair*
ar as in *car*
ard as in *hard*
ark as in *park*
arm as in *farm*
art as in *cart*
as as in *base*
as as in *gas*
ash as in *dash*
ask as in *mask*

ast as in *paste*
ast as in *last*
at as in *gate*
at as in *fat*
ath as in *math*
av as in *gave*
az as in *days*
az as in *jazz*

e as in *fee*
ech as in *teach*
ed as in *bead*
ed as in *head*
ef as in *beef*
ef as in *deaf*
eg as in *leg*
ek as in *week*

195

e

ek as in *neck*
el as in *heal*
el as in *fell*
eld as in *yelled*
elf as in *self*
elt as in *melt*
em as in *seam*
em as in *hem*
en as in *mean*
en as in *pen*
end as in *send*
ens as in *fence*
ent as in *tent*
ep as in *keep*
er as in *dear*
es as in *geese*
es as in *guess*
est as in *feast*
est as in *test*
et as in *feet*
et as in *jet*
ex as in *necks*
ez as in *keys*

I

i as in *pie*
ib as in *rib*
ich as in *rich*
id as in *ride*
id as in *did*
if as in *life*
ift as in *gift*
ig as in *fig*
ik as in *like*
ik as in *lick*
iks as in *fix*
il as in *mile*
il as in *hill*
ild as in *wild*
ild as in *filled*
im as in *dime*
im as in *him*
in as in *line*
in as in *pin*
ind as in *kind*
ind as in *pinned*
ing as in *sing*
ink as in *sink*
inks as in *winks*
ins as in *since*
int as in *mint*

ip as in *ripe*
ip as in *dip*
ir as in *tire*
is as in *rice*
is as in *miss*
ish as in *wish*
ist as in *list*
it as in *kite*
it as in *sit*
iv as in *five*
iz as in *pies*
iz as in *his*

O

o as in *go*
ob as in *job*
od as in *road*
og as in *fog*
oi as in *toy*
oil as in *soil*
ois as in *voice*
oiz as in *noise*
ok as in *joke*
ok as in *lock*
oks as in *fox*
ol as in *hole*
ol as in *fall*

old as in *fold*
olk as in *walk*
om as in *home*
om as in *mom*
on as in *bone*
on as in *lawn*
ond as in *bond*
ong as in *long*
oo as in *few*
oo as in *zoo*
ood as in *good*
ood as in *mood*
oof as in *roof*
ook as in *cook*
ool as in *cool*
oom as in *room*
oon as in *moon*
oop as in *soup*
oos as in *moose*
oot as in *suit*
ooth as in *tooth*
oov as in *you've*
ooz as in *lose*
op as in *soap*
op as in *hop*
or as in *pour*
ord as in *roared*
orn as in *corn*
ors as in *horse*

ort as in *fort*
os as in *loss*
ost as in *most*
ost as in *cost*
ot as in *goat*
ot as in *hot*
ot as in *taught*
ow as in *cow*
owch as in *pouch*
owd as in *loud*
own as in *down*
ownd as in *found*
owr as in *sour*
ows as in *house*
owt as in *pout*
oz as in *nose*

u as in *zoo*
u as in *few*
ub as in *rub*
uch as in *such*
ud as in *mood*
ud as in *mud*
udj as in *fudge*
uf as in *roof*
uf as in *cuff*

ug as in *rug*
uk as in *duck*

ul as in *cool*
ul as in *full*
um as in *room*
um as in *gum*
ump as in *jump*
un as in *moon*
un as in *fun*
unch as in *lunch*
ung as in *young*
unk as in *junk*
up as in *soup*
up as in *pup*
ur as in *fur*
urch as in *search*
urd as in *herd*
urk as in *work*
url as in *girl*
urld as in *world*
urm as in *germ*
urn as in *learn*
urs as in *verse*
urst as in *first*

U

urt as in *dirt*

us as in *moose*

us as in *bus*

ush as in *push*

ush as in *rush*

usk as in *tusk*

ust as in *must*

ut as in *suit*

ut as in *cut*

ut as in *put*

uth as in *tooth*

uv as in *you've*

uv as in *love*

uz as in *lose*

uz as in *fuzz*

Index of Synonyms

abandon (see *stop*)

abandoned (see *empty; went*)

abhor (see *hate*)

about (see *almost*)

abruptly (see *suddenly*)

absolutely (see *very*)

absurd (see *crazy*)

abused (see *hurt*)

accelerate (see *hurry*)

accept (see *take*)

accomplished (see *won*)

accurate (see *right; true*)

accuse (see *blame*)

achieved (see *won*)

acquaintance (see *friend*)

acquire (see *have; take*)

acres (see *lots*)

active (see *busy*)

added (see *said*)

address (see *home; talk*)

admire (see *love*)

admit (see *let*)

admitted (see *said*)

admonished (see *said*)

adopt (see *choose*)

adore (see *love*)

advanced (see *went*)

adventure (see *story*)

aerial (see *tall*)

affluent (see *rich*)

afraid (see *scared*)

aged (see *old*)

agreeable (see *new; ready*)

aid (see *help*)

ailing (see *sick*)

airy (see *light*)

alarmed (see *scared*)

alarming (see *dangerous*)

alike, 10

a

alive (see *excited*)

all right (see *good; safe*)

alley (see *street*)

allow (see *let*)

almost, 10

alone (see *lonely*)

altogether (see *very*)

ambled (see *walked; went*)

ample (see *fat; full*)

amputate (see *cut*)

amusement (see *fun*)

amusing (see *funny; interesting*)

ancestors (see *family*)

ancient (see *old*)

angry, 10

announced (see *said*)

annoy (see *bother*)

answer, 10

answered (see *said*)

ant-sized (see *little*)

antique (see *old*)

anxious (see *worried*)

AOK (see *good*)

apartment (see *home*)

aplenty (see *lots*)

appealing (see *pretty*)

appear (see *come*)

apprehensive (see *shy; worried*)

approach (see *come*)

appropriate (see *good; new*)

approve of (see *let*)

argue, 10

argued (see *said*)

arid (see *dry*)

army (see *lots*)

around (see *almost*)

arrive (see *come*)

ashamed, 11

ask, 11

assemble (see *build*)

assignment (see *work*)

assist (see *help*)

assorted (see *different*)

attempt (see *try*)

attractive (see *interesting; pretty*)

authentic (see *true*)

authorize (see *let*)

automobile (see *car*)

available (see *ready*)

avenue (see *street*)

average (see *mean*)

awesome (see *big*)

awful (see *bad; wrong*)

awfully (see *very*)

background (see *family*)

bad, 11

bad-looking (see *ugly*)

baffled (see *confused*)

bankrupt (see *poor*)

barbaric (see *mean*)

bare (see *dry*)

bash (see *hit*)

bashful (see *shy*)

bathed (see *clean*)

battle (see *argue*)

batty (see *crazy*)

bawl (see *cry*)

bawled (see *said*)

beat (see *thin*)

beat it (see *run*)

beat up (see *hit*)

beautiful (see *pretty*)

becoming (see *pretty*)

bedlam (see *noise*)

bedtime (see *night*)

beg (see *ask*)

begin, 11

beginning (see *first*)

beheld (see *saw*)

believe, 11

bellow (see *shout*)

bellyache (see *complain*)

below (see *under*)

beneath (see *under*)

best (see *good*)

bevy (see *crowd*)

bewail (see *complain*)

bewildered (see *confused*)

big, 12

big (see *fat*)

big cheese (see *famous*)

bill (see *money*)

bind (see *join*)

biography (see *story*)

bitter (see *cold*)

blah (see *boring*)

blame, 12

blank (see *empty*)

blaring (see *loud*)

blissful (see *happy*)

b

bustle (see *hurry*)
bustling (see *busy; excited*)
busy, 14
buy, 14

cabin (see *home*)
caboose (see *car; last*)
cackle (see *laugh*)
called (see *said*)
calm (see *quiet*)
canter (see *run*)
capture (see *catch*)
car, 14
career (see *work*)
carry, 14

cart (see *carry*)
carve (see *cut*)
castle (see *home*)

catch, 14
catnap (see *sleep*)
cautioned (see *said*)
cavernous (see *deep*)
cease (see *stop*)
celebrate, 15
celebrated (see *famous*)
center (see *mean*)
challenged (see *said*)
chancy (see *dangerous*)
change, 15
change (see *money*)
char (see *burn*)
charming (see *interesting*)
chase, 15
chatter (see *talk*)
cheat, 15
cheer (see *shout*)
cheerful (see *happy*)
cheerless (see *sad*)
cherish (see *love*)
chic (see *pretty*)
chief (see *first*)
chiefly (see *very*)
childlike (see *young*)
children (see *family*)
chilly (see *cold*)
choose, 15
chore (see *work*)

chortle (see *laugh*)

chubby (see *fat*)

chuckle (see *laugh*)

chum (see *friend*)

chunk (see *part*)

cinch (see *easy*)

claimed (see *said*)

classmate (see *friend*)

clean, 16

clear, 16

clever (see *smart*)

clinging vine (see *shy*)

closing (see *last*)

cloudburst (see *storm*)

cloudless (see *clear*)

coarse (see *rough*)

cobble (see *fix*)

coins (see *money*)

cold, 16

cold-blooded (see *mean*)

collapse (see *fall*)

come, 17

comfortable (see *soft*)

comical (see *funny*)

commented (see *said*)

commotion (see *noise*)

communicate (see *talk; write*)

companion (see *friend*)

companionless (see *lonely*)

complain, 17

complete (see *stop*)

completely (see *very*)

compose (see *write*)

comprehend (see *understand*)

con (see *cheat; steal*)

concerned (see *worried*)

concluding (see *last*)

condominium (see *home*)

confused, 17

conk (see *hit*)

connect (see *join*)

conquered (see *won*)

consider (see *try*)

considerably (see *very*)

consolidate (see *join*)

construct (see *build*)

consume (see *eat*)

contemporary (see *new*)

contented (see *happy*)

contrasting (see *different*)

converse (see *talk*)

convertible (see *car*)

cool (see *pretty*)

cooled (see *cold*)

core (see *mean*)

correct (see *fix; good; new; right; true*)

corrupt (see *wrong*)

cottage (see *home*)

couple (see *join*)

courageous (see *brave*)

covet (see *want*)

crab (see *complain*)

crack (see *break*)

crash (see *sleep*)

crave (see *want*)

crazed (see *crazy*)

crazy, 18

cream (see *hit*)

create (see *build*)

cried (see *said*)

criminal (see *bad; wrong*)

crinkly (see *rough*)

crisp (see *cold*)

criticize (see *blame*)

croaked (see *said*)

crooked (see *bad*)

cross (see *angry*)

crowd, 18

crowded (see *full*)

cruel (see *mean*)

crumb (see *part*)

crummy (see *sad*)

crumple (see *fall*)

crushed (see *sad*)

cry, 18

curious, 18

curry (see *rub*)

cushiony (see *soft*)

cut, 19

cute (see *pretty*)

cyclone (see *storm*)

D

damage (see *break*)

damaged (see *hurt*)

damp (see *wet*)

dangerous, 19

daring (see *brave*)

Index of Synonyms

d

dark, 19
darkness (see *night*)
dart (see *run*)
dash (see *run*)
dawdling (see *slow*)
dazzling (see *bright*)
dead, 19
dead-center (see *mean*)
dead-tired (see *tired*)
deafening (see *loud*)
debate (see *argue*)
deceased (see *dead*)
deceive (see *cheat*)
declare (see *talk*)
declared (see *said*)
dedicate (see *begin; celebrate*)
deduce (see *understand*)
deep, 20
deepen (see *grow*)
dehydrated (see *dry*)
delayed (see *late*)
delicate (see *light; weak*)
delicious (see *good*)
delight (see *fun*)
delighted (see *happy*)
delightful (see *new; pretty*)
deliver (see *carry*)
demanded (see *said*)
demanding (see *hard*)

demolish (see *break*)
depart (see *run*)
departed (see *dead; went*)
dependable (see *true*)
deposit (see *money*)
depressed (see *sad*)
descended (see *went*)
described (see *said*)
deserted (see *empty; went*)
desire (see *want*)
desirous (see *jealous*)
despise (see *hate*)
destroy (see *break*)
detect (see *find*)
detest (see *hate*)
develop (see *build; grow*)
developed (see *full*)
devour (see *eat*)
different, 20

difficult, 20
diluted (see *weak*)
dim (see *dark*)
dine (see *eat*)

dinky (see *little*)

dinosaur (see *old*)

dippy (see *crazy*)

dirty, 21

disagree (see *argue*)

disappeared (see *went*)

discontinue (see *stop*)

discouraged (see *sad*)

discover (see *find*)

diseased (see *sick*)

disfigured (see *ugly*)

dishonest (see *bad*)

dislike (see *hate*)

dismal (see *dark*)

displeasing (see *ugly*)

dissect (see *cut*)

distinctive (see *different*)

distinguished (see *famous*)

disturb (see *bother*)

disturbed (see *confused; worried*)

divide (see *cut*)

dog-tired (see *tired*)

dollar (see *money*)

dormant (see *dead*)

double (see *grow*)

dough (see *money*)

downcast (see *sad*)

downhearted (see *sad*)

downpour (see *storm*)

downright (see *very*)

doze (see *sleep*)

dragster (see *car*)

dreary (see *boring; dark*)

drenched (see *wet*)

driveway (see *street*)

drop (see *fall*)

drove (see *crowd*)

drowsy (see *thin*)

dry, 21

dull (see *boring; dark*)

durable (see *strong*)

dusk (see *night*)

dusted (see *clean*)

dusty (see *dirty*)

duty (see *work*)

dwarfed (see *little*)

dynasty (see *family*)

eager (see *excited*)

earliest (see *first*)

earsplitting (see *loud*)

earthshaking (see *loud*)

easy, 21

eat, 22

ecstatic (see *happy*)

effort (see *work*)

elated (see *happy*)

elderly (see *old*)

elect (see *choose*)

elementary (see *easy*)

elephant-sized (see *big*)

elevated (see *high; tall*)

embarrassed (see *ashamed*)

employment (see *work*)

empty, 22

enchanting (see *interesting*)

end (see *last; stop*)

ending (see *last*)

energetic (see *excited*)

enjoy (see *love*)

enjoyable (see *interesting; new*)

enjoyment (see *fun*)

enlarge (see *grow*)

enormous (see *big*)

enormously (see *very*)

entertaining (see *funny; interesting*)

entertainment (see *fun*)

enthusiastic (see *excited*)

entirely (see *very*)

envious (see *jealous*)

equal (see *alike*)

erect (see *build*)

errand (see *work*)

escaped (see *went*)

especially (see *very*)

esteemed (see *famous*)

evening (see *night*)

evil (see *bad; dark; mean*)

exact (see *right*)

examined (see *saw*)

exceedingly (see *very*)

excelled (see *won*)

excellent (see *good*)

excess of (see *lots*)

f

excited, 22
excitement (see *fun*)
exciting (see *interesting*)
exclaim (see *shout*)
exclaimed (see *said*)
exhausted (see *thin*)
exhausting (see *difficult*)
expand (see *grow*)
explain (see *answer*)
explained (see *said*)
express (see *talk*)
extinct (see *dead; old*)
extra (see *lots*)
extraordinarily (see *very*)
extraordinary (see *different; new*)
extremely (see *very*)
eye-catching (see *pretty*)
eyed (see *saw*)

fable (see *story*)
factual (see *true*)
faint (see *dark; weak*)
fair (see *pretty; right*)
fall, 23
family, 23

famished (see *hungry*)
famous, 23
fancy (see *want*)
fantasy (see *story*)
fascinating (see *interesting*)
fast, 24

fat, 24
fathom (see *understand*)
fatigued (see *thin*)
fearful (see *scared; worried*)
fearless (see *brave*)
feast (see *eat*)
feathery (see *light*)
feeble (see *weak*)
fetch (see *carry*)
feverish (see *hot*)
fiery (see *hot*)
filled (see *full*)
filthy (see *dirty*)
final (see *last*)
find, 24
fine (see *good; pretty*)
finish (see *stop*)

f

first, 24
fix, 25
flaming (see *hot*)
flat (see *smooth*)
flawed (see *wrong*)
flawless (see *right; true*)
fled (see *went*)
flee (see *run*)
flew (see *went*)
flexible (see *soft*)
flimsy (see *weak*)
flock (see *crowd*)
flourish (see *grow*)
flustered (see *confused*)
focus (see *mean*)
folk tale (see *story*)
folks (see *family*)
follow (see *chase*)
foolish (see *crazy*)
foremost (see *first*)
forlorn (see *lonely; sad*)
fortissimo (see *loud*)
fossil (see *old*)
foul (see *dirty*)
fraction (see *part*)
fragile (see *weak*)
frail (see *weak*)
freeway (see *street*)
freezing (see *cold*)

frequently (see *often*)
fresh (see *clean; new; young*)
fretful (see *worried*)
friend, 25

friendless (see *lonely*)
friendly (see *new*)
frightened (see *scared*)
frosted (see *cold*)
frosty (see *cold*)
full, 25
full-grown (see *tall*)
fume (see *complain*)
fun, 25
fun (see *interesting*)
funny, 26
furious (see *angry*)

gain (see *come; take*)
gallop (see *run*)

gasped (see *said*)

gather (see *take*)

gaunt (see *thin*)

genuine (see *true*)

germinate (see *grow*)

gigantic (see *big*)

giggle (see *laugh*)

glad (see *happy*)

glamorous (see *pretty*)

gleeful (see *happy*)

glimpsed (see *saw*)

glistening (see *shiny*)

gloat (see *brag*)

gloomy (see *dark; sad*)

glossy (see *shiny*)

glowing (see *bright; shiny*)

gobs (see *lots*)

gone (see *dead*)

good, 26

good-looking (see *pretty*)

good-natured (see *happy*)

goofy (see *crazy*)

gorge (see *eat*)

gorgeous (see *pretty*)

grab (see *catch*)

grasp (see *catch; take; understand*)

great (see *big; famous; good*)

grimy (see *dirty*)

grip (see *take*)

gripe (see *complain*)

groom (see *rub*)

grouch (see *complain*)

grow, 27

growl (see *complain*)

grumble (see *complain*)

guarded (see *safe*)

guffaw (see *laugh*)

guilty (see *ashamed*)

gung-ho (see *excited*)

gutsy (see *brave*)

H

hair-raising (see *scared*)

half-baked (see *poor*)

halt (see *stop*)

hammer (see *hit*)

happy, 27

hard, 28

hard (see *difficult*)

hardy (see *strong*)

harmed (see *hurt*)

harmful (see *bad*)

harmless (see *safe*)

harsh (see *loud*)

hasten (see *hurry*)

hate, 28

h

hurdle (see *jump*)

hurricane (see *storm*)

hurriedly (see *suddenly*)

hurry, 30

hurt, 30

hurtful (see *mean*)

hushed (see *quiet*)

husky (see *fat*)

hustle (see *hurry; steal*)

hyped (see *excited*)

iced (see *cold*)

icy (see *cold*)

idiotic (see *crazy*)

idle (see *lazy*)

idolize (see *love*)

ill (see *sick*)

illegal (see *wrong*)

immature (see *young*)

immediately (see *suddenly*)

immoral (see *wrong*)

improper (see *wrong*)

improve (see *change*)

inaccurate (see *wrong*)

inactive (see *lazy*)

income (see *money*)

incorrect (see *wrong*)

increase (see *grow*)

indigent (see *poor*)

informed (see *said*)

inhuman (see *mean*)

initial (see *first*)

injured (see *hurt*)

inorganic (see *dead*)

inquire (see *ask*)

inquiring (see *curious*)

inquisitive (see *curious*)

insane (see *crazy*)

inspected (see *saw*)

instantly (see *suddenly*)

intelligent (see *smart*)

intense (see *loud*)

interesting, 31

intimidated (see *scared*)

investigative (see *curious*)

invite (see *ask*)

inviting (see *interesting*)

involved (see *busy*)

invulnerable (see *safe*)

irrational (see *crazy; wrong*)
irregular (see *rough*)
irritate (see *bother*)
isolated (see *lonely*)
itching (see *jealous*)
itty-bitty (see *little*)

jagged (see *rough*)
jam (see *crowd*)
jam-packed (see *full*)
jealous, 31
job (see *work*)
jog (see *run*)
join, 31
jolly (see *happy*)
jot (see *write*)
journeyed (see *went*)
joyful (see *happy*)
joyless (see *sad*)
jubilant (see *happy*)
jump, 31
just (see *right*)

keen (see *smart*)
keep, 32
keyed-up (see *excited*)
kin (see *family*)
kind (see *new*)
knead (see *rub*)
knock (see *hit*)

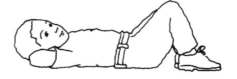

lane (see *street*)
lanky (see *thin*)
large (see *big; fat*)
last, 32
late, 32
latest (see *last; new*)
laugh, 32
laughable (see *funny*)
laughed (see *said*)
laundered (see *clean*)
lawful (see *right*)
lazy, 33

leading (see *first*)

lean (see *thin*)

leap (see *jump*)

leave (see *run*)

legal (see *right*)

legend (see *story*)

legitimate (see *true*)

lengthen (see *grow*)

let, 33

licensed (see *right*)

lied (see *said*)

lifeless (see *boring; cold; dead*)

light, 33

lighthearted (see *happy*)

lightless (see *dark*)

lightning-swift (see *fast*)

likable (see *new*)

like (see *love*)

limousine (see *car*)

link (see *join*)

listless (see *lazy*)

little, 33

loaded (see *rich*)

loads (see *lots*)

loathe (see *hate*)

locate (see *find*)

lofty (see *high*)

lofty (see *tall*)

logical (see *right*)

lonely, 33

lonesome (see *lonely*)

long (see *want*)

loony (see *crazy*)

lope (see *run*)

lot (see *often*)

lots, 34

loud, 34

love, 34

lovely (see *pretty*)

lug (see *carry*)

M

mad (see *angry; crazy*)

magnificent (see *good; pretty*)

magnify (see *grow*)

main (see *first*)

mainly (see *very*)

major (see *first*)

make (see *build*)

manufacture (see *build*)

many (see *lots*)

marry (see *join*)

massage (see *rub*)

masses (see *lots*)

massive (see *fat*)

mature (see *grow*)

m

mean, 35

mean (see *middle*)

median (see *mean*)

meet (see *join*)

mend (see *fix*)

mentioned (see *said*)

merge (see *join*)

merry (see *happy*)

messy (see *dirty*)

middle, 35

midpoint (see *mean*)

mighty (see *strong; very*)

migrated (see *went*)

mind-boggling (see *difficult*)

mini (see *little*)

miniature (see *little*)

minor (see *little; young*)

miserable (see *sad*)

mislead (see *cheat*)

mistaken (see *wrong*)

mistreated (see *hurt*)

mixed-up (see *wrong*)

moan (see *cry*)

mob (see *crowd*)

modern (see *new*)

moist (see *wet*)

mold (see *build*)

money, 35

monsoon (see *storm*)

monstrous (see *big*)

moral (see *right*)

mostly (see *very*)

mouthed (see *said*)

much (see *lots*)

muddy (see *dirty*)

multiply (see *grow*)

murmured (see *said*)

myth (see *story*)

nag (see *complain*)

nap (see *sleep*)

narrative (see *story*)

narrow (see *thin*)

nasty (see *bad; ugly*)

natural (see *easy; true*)

nearly (see *almost*)

neat (see *pretty*)

need (see *want*)

needy (see *poor*)

neighborly (see *new*)

nervous (see *worried*)

net (see *catch*)

netted (see *won*)

never, 36

new, 36

nice, 36

night, 36

nighttime (see *night*)

nimble (see *light*)

noise, 37

noisy (see *loud*)

nonfictional (see *true*)

nonsensical (see *crazy*)

nosy (see *curious*)

note (see *write*)

noted (see *saw*)

notice (see *find*)

noticed (see *saw*)

novel (see *story*)

nucleus (see *mean*)

numb (see *dead*)

nurse (see *help*)

O

obedient (see *good*)

obese (see *fat*)

observe (see *celebrate*)

observed (see *saw*)

obtain (see *take*)

obvious (see *clear; easy*)

occupied (see *busy*)

odd (see *different*)

offered (see *said*)

official (see *true*)

oft (see *often*)

often, 37

okay (see *good; safe*)

old, 37

old-fashioned (see *old*)

oodles (see *lots*)

open (see *begin*)

opening (see *first*)

opera (see *story*)

optimistic (see *happy*)

ordered (see *said*)

original (see *first*)

outdated (see *old*)

outstanding (see *big; good*)

outwit (see *cheat*)

over the hill (see *old*)

overdue (see *late*)

overflowing (see *full*)

overjoyed (see *happy*)

overweight (see *fat*)

own (see *have*)

paced (see *walked*)

packed (see *full*)

pad (see *home*)

padded (see *walked*)

pained (see *hurt*)

pal (see *friend*)

pandemonium (see *noise*)

panted (see *said*)

parched (see *dry*)

part, 38

particle (see *part*)

particularly (see *very*)

passed (see *went*)

passive (see *quiet*)

pat (see *rub*)

patch (see *fix*)

pavement (see *street*)

pay (see *money*)

peaceful (see *quiet*)

pedigree (see *family*)

peer (see *friend*)

peewee (see *little*)

pen (see *write*)

pencil-thin (see *thin*)

penniless (see *poor*)

people (see *family*)

perceived (see *saw*)

perfect (see *good; right; true*)

periodically (see *often*)

perished (see *dead*)

permit (see *let*)

pester (see *bother*)

pet (see *rub*)

pick (see *choose; take*)

pictured (see *saw*)

piece (see *part*)

pinpoint (see *find*)

pit (see *dirty*)

plain (see *clear; easy*)

play (see *fun; story*)

playmate (see *friend*)

plead (see *ask*)

pleaded (see *said*)

pleasant (see *new*)

pleased (see *happy*)

pleasing (see *pretty*)

pleasure (see *fun*)

plodded (see *walked*)

plodding (see *slow*)

plump (see *fat*)

plunder (see *steal*)

p

plush (see *soft*)

point out (see *talk*)

pointless (see *boring*)

polar (see *cold*)

polish (see *rub*)

polished (see *clean; shiny; smooth*)

polite (see *new*)

poor, 38

poor (see *bad*)

popular (see *famous*)

portion (see *part*)

positive (see *happy*)

possess (see *have; take*)

postponed (see *late*)

pounce (see *jump*)

pound (see *hit*)

poverty-stricken (see *poor*)

powerful (see *strong*)

praised (see *said*)

praiseworthy (see *good*)

pranced (see *walked*)

preached (see *said*)

precise (see *right*)

prefer (see *want*)

prehistoric (see *old*)

premiere (see *first*)

prepare (see *fix*)

prepared (see *ready*)

preposterous (see *crazy*)

preserve (see *keep*)

pretty, 38

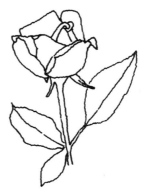

prevent (see *help*)

primarily (see *very*)

primary (see *first*)

primed (see *ready*)

proceeded (see *went*)

produce (see *build*)

project (see *work*)

promised (see *said*)

promptly (see *suddenly*)

proper (see *new; true*)

proposed (see *said*)

prosper (see *grow*)

prosperous (see *rich*)

protect (see *keep*)

protected (see *safe*)

prune (see *cut*)

puny (see *weak*)

purchase (see *buy*)

pure (see *clean*)
pursue (see *chase*)
pushover (see *weak*)
puzzling (see *difficult*)

Q

quarrel (see *argue*)
question (see *ask*)
questioning (see *curious*)
quick (see *fast*)
quickly (see *suddenly*)
quiet, 39

quit (see *stop*)
quite (see *very*)

race (see *hurry; run*)
racket (see *noise*)

radiant (see *shiny*)
rambled (see *went*)
ranted (see *said*)
rap (see *talk*)
rapid (see *fast*)
rapidly (see *suddenly*)
rarely (see *never*)
rational (see *right*)
ravenous (see *hungry*)
reach (see *come*)
ready, 39
real (see *true*)
realize (see *understand*)
realized (see *saw*)
reaped (see *won*)
rearmost (see *last*)
reasonable (see *right*)
receive (see *catch; take*)
recent (see *new; young*)
recited (see *said*)
record (see *write*)
recreation (see *fun*)
red-faced (see *ashamed*)
refrigerated (see *cold*)
regularly (see *often*)
relatives (see *family*)
reluctant (see *shy*)
remarked (see *said*)
remedy (see *fix*)

reminded (see *said*)

remote (see *cold*)

repair (see *fix*)

replied (see *said*)

reply (see *answer*)

reported (see *said*)

repulsive (see *ugly*)

request (see *ask*)

rescue (see *help*)

reserve (see *keep*)

residence (see *home*)

respected (see *famous*)

respond (see *answer*)

responded (see *said*)

restless (see *thin*)

restore (see *fix*)

retire (see *sleep*)

retreat (see *run*)

retreated (see *went*)

rich, 39

riches (see *money*)

ridiculous (see *funny*)

right, 39

rigid (see *hard*)

rip (see *cut*)

risky (see *dangerous*)

road (see *street*)

roamed (see *walked*)

roar (see *laugh; shout*)

roared (see *said*)

roaring (see *loud*)

roasting (see *hot*)

rob (see *steal*)

roots (see *family*)

rotten (see *bad*)

rough, 40

route (see *street*)

rub, 40

ruckus (see *noise*)

rude (see *bad*)

rugged (see *strong*)

ruin (see *break*)

ruined (see *hurt*)

run, 40

rush (see *hurry; run*)

S

sad, 41
safe, 41
said, 42

salary (see *money*)

salvage (see *keep*)

same (see *alike*)

sample (see *try*)

sanded (see *smooth*)

sandstorm (see *storm*)

Index of Synonyms

S

satisfied (see *happy*)

saturated (see *wet*)

savage (see *mean*)

save (see *keep*)

savings (see *money*)

saw, 43

say (see *talk*)

scads (see *lots*)

scamper (see *run*)

scant (see *little*)

scared, 43

schoolwork (see *work*)

scold (see *blame*)

scoot (see *run*)

scorch (see *burn*)

scored (see *won*)

scour (see *rub*)

scoured (see *clean*)

scramble (see *run*)

scrammed (see *went*)

scrap (see *part*)

scrawny (see *thin*)

scream (see *shout*)

screamed (see *said*)

scribble (see *write*)

scrub (see *rub*)

scrubbed (see *clean*)

scurry (see *hurry; run*)

seamless (see *smooth*)

searching (see *curious*)

section (see *part*)

secure (see *safe*)

segment (see *part*)

seize (see *catch*)

select (see *choose*)

separate (see *lonely*)

serve (see *help*)

shadowy (see *dark*)

shaky (see *weak*)

share (see *part*)

sharp (see *smart*)

shave (see *cut*)

sheepish (see *ashamed*)

shelter (see *home*)

sheltered (see *safe*)

shiny, 44

shiny (see *bright; clean*)

shivering (see *cold*)

shoplift (see *steal*)

short (see *little*)

222

shout, 44

shouted (see *said*)

shrieked (see *said*)

shuffled (see *walked*)

shy, 44

sick, 44

side-splitting (see *funny*)

sidekick (see *friend*)

sighed (see *said*)

sighted (see *saw*)

silent (see *quiet*)

silly (see *crazy; funny*)

similar (see *alike*)

simple (see *easy*)

sincere (see *true*)

sink (see *fall*)

skedaddle (see *hurry*)

skeletal (see *thin*)

skinny (see *thin*)

slap (see *hit*)

slash (see *cut*)

sleep, 44

sleepy (see *tired*)

slender (see *thin*)

slice (see *cut; part*)

slide (see *fall*)

slight (see *light*)

slim (see *thin*)

slip (see *cut; fall*)

slit (see *cut*)

slow, 45

sluggish (see *slow*)

slumber (see *sleep*)

slump (see *fall*)

smack (see *hit*)

small (see *little*)

smart, 45

smash (see *break*)

smirked (see *said*)

smolder (see *burn*)

smooth, 45

smothered (see *dead*)

snack (see *eat*)

snail-like (see *slow*)

snapped (see *said*)

snatch (see *catch*)

snicker (see *laugh*)

snitch (see *steal*)

snivel (see *cry*)

snoopy (see *curious*)

snooze (see *sleep*)

snowball (see *grow*)

snowfall (see *storm*)

soaked (see *wet*)

S

streetcar (see *car*)

stretch (see *grow*)

strike (see *hit*)

striking (see *pretty*)

strip (see *street*)

strode (see *walked*)

stroke (see *rub*)

strolled (see *walked*)

strong, 47

strutted (see *walked*)

stuffed (see *full*)

stumble (see *fall*)

stunning (see *pretty*)

stupid (see *crazy*)

sturdy (see *strong*)

stuttered (see *said*)

stylish (see *pretty*)

submerged in (see *under*)

substitute (see *change*)

succeeded (see *won*)

suddenly, 47

suffocated (see *dead*)

suggested (see *said*)

suitable (see *good; new*)

sultry (see *hot*)

summon (see *ask*)

sunny (see *bright; happy*)

sunset (see *night*)

super (see *good*)

superb (see *good*)

superhighway (see *street*)

superior (see *good*)

support (see *help*)

surveyed (see *saw*)

swaggered (see *walked*)

swarm (see *crowd*)

sweating (see *hot*)

swell (see *grow*)

sweltering (see *hot*)

swept (see *clean; won*)

swift (see *fast*)

swiftly (see *suddenly*)

swindle (see *steal*)

switch (see *change*)

take, 47

tale (see *story*)

talk, 48

tall, 48

tardy (see *late*)

task (see *work*)

taste (see *try*)

taut (see *hard*)

taxicab (see *car*)

teammate (see *friend*)

tear (see *break; cut*)

tearful (see *sad*)

tease (see *bother*)

tedious (see *difficult*)

tee-hee (see *laugh*)

teeny (see *little*)

tell (see *answer*)

tempting (see *interesting*)

tense (see *hard*)

tent (see *home*)

terminated (see *dead*)

terrible (see *bad*)

terribly (see *very*)

terrified (see *scared*)

test (see *try*)

thicken (see *grow*)

thieve (see *steal*)

thin, 48

thirsty (see *dry*)

thoroughfare (see *street*)

thoroughly (see *very*)

thought-provoking (see *interesting*)

thoughtful (see *new*)

threadlike (see *thin*)

thrilled (see *happy*)

thrive (see *grow*)

throng (see *crowd*)

thump (see *hit*)

thunderous (see *loud*)

tidy (see *clean*)

tie (see *join*)

timid (see *shy*)

tiny (see *light; little*)

tiptoed (see *walked*)

tired, 49

tired (see *dead*)

tiresome (see *dry*)

tiring (see *boring*)

titter (see *laugh*)

told (see *said*)

toll road (see *street*)

tons (see *lots*)

topple (see *fall*)

tops (see *good*)

torn (see *confused*)

tornado (see *storm*)

torrid (see *hot*)

totally (see *very*)

tote (see *carry*)

tottered (see *walked*)

tough (see *strong*)

towering (see *high; tall*)

townhouse (see *home*)

track (see *chase*)

trade (see *change*)

trail (see *chase*)

trailer (see *home*)

tranquil (see *quiet*)

transport (see *carry*)

trap (see *catch*)

traveled (see *went*)

treacherous (see *dangerous*)

treasure (see *love*)

trekked (see *walked; went*)

tribe (see *family*)

trick (see *cheat*)

trim (see *cut*)

trip (see *fall*)

trolley (see *car*)

trot (see *run*)

troubled (see *confused; worried*)

troubling (see *difficult*)

trudged (see *walked*)

true, 49

trust (see *believe*)

trusted (see *true*)

trustworthy (see *good*)

try, 49

trying (see *difficult*)

tuckered out (see *thin*)

tumble (see *fall*)

turmoil (see *noise*)

turnpike (see *street*)

twilight (see *night*)

twin (see *alike*)

typhoon (see *storm*)

ugly, 50

umpteen (see *lots*)

unafraid (see *brave*)

unappealing (see *ugly*)

unattractive (see *ugly*)

unbalanced (see *crazy*)

unbending (see *hard*)

uncertain (see *confused*)

unclean (see *dirty*)

uncommonly (see *very*)

uncomplicated (see *easy*)

uncover (see *find*)

undamaged (see *safe*)

under, 50

underneath (see *under*)

understand, 50

understood (see *saw*)

undertake (see *try*)

undeveloped (see *young*)

uneasy (see *worried*)

uneven (see *rough*)

unfamiliar (see *new*)

unfeeling (see *mean*)

unfriendly (see *cold*)

unfulfilled (see *empty*)

unfurnished (see *empty*)

unhappy (see *sad*)

unhealthy (see *sick*)

uninteresting (see *boring*)

unique (see *different*)

uniquely (see *very*)

unite (see *join*)

unlawful (see *wrong*)

unlike (see *different*)

unmotivated (see *lazy*)

unpleasant (see *ugly*)

unsafe (see *dangerous*)

unsightly (see *ugly*)

unstable (see *weak*)

untroubled (see *happy*)

untrue (see *wrong*)

unusual (see *different; new*)

unusually (see *very*)

unwell (see *sick*)

unyielding (see *hard*)

up-to-the-minute (see *new*)

upbeat (see *happy*)

uproar (see *noise*)

upset (see *confused; worried*)

used (see *old*)

usually (see *often*)

utter (see *talk*)

uttered (see *said*)

vacant (see *empty*)

vacuumed (see *clean*)

valid (see *true*)

value (see *believe*)

vamoosed (see *went*)

van (see *car*)

varying (see *different*)

vault (see *jump*)

vehicle (see *car*)

very, 51

vicious (see *mean*)

viewed (see *saw*)

volumes (see *lots*)

volunteered (see *said*)

wacko (see *crazy*)

waddled (see *walked*)

wail (see *cry*)

walked, 51

wandered (see *walked; went*)

want, 52

warned (see *said*)

washed (see *clean*)

watched (see *saw*)

weak, 52

wealth (see *money*)

wealthy (see *rich*)

weary (see *thin*)

wee (see *little*)

weep (see *cry*)

weightless (see *light*)

well-behaved (see *good*)

well-known (see *famous*)

well-mannered (see *good*)

well-off (see *rich*)

went, 52

wept (see *said*)

wet, 53

whack (see *hit*)

whimper (see *cry*)

whine (see *cry*)

whispered (see *said*)

wicked (see *mean*)

wide (see *fat*)

Index